My faith in Jesus as Lord and Savior . . . is a conviction certified from above and within rather than from evidence observable by anyone. Just what I mean by this 'truth' is always partial and incomplete, subject to ever new depths of insight and understanding.

Lutherans and Catholics in Dialogue

Personal Notes for a Study

By Paul C. Empie

Edited by Raymond Tiemeyer

Fortress Press, Philadelphia

LUTHERANS AND CATHOLICS IN DIALOGUE

Designed by Judith I. Gotwald.

Library of Congress Cataloging in Publication Data

Empie, Paul C
Lutherans and Catholics in dialogue.

1. Lutheran Church—Relations—Catholic Church—Study and teaching. 2. Catholic Church—Relations—Lutheran Church—Study and teaching. 3. Theology, Doctrinal—Study and teaching. I. Tiemeyer, Raymond. II. Title.
Bx8063.7.C3E47 230'.2 80-69754
ISBN 0-8006-1449-6

8866I80 Printed in U.S.A. 1-1449

CONTENTS

FOREWORD

In terms of the centuries that have separated Lutherans and Catholics, January 1965 is certainly not long ago. It was then that the author of this book came to see me to discuss what was to be the first of the official bilateral dialogues between theologians of the Roman Catholic Church and other Christian communions in the United States. Considering the better mutual understanding gained by these dialogues, in terms of the common confessions we have been able to make to our faith in Christ Jesus as the Lord, it would seem that much more time would have passed since the day of that meeting. That this was not so has been due to the response to the grace of our Lord Jesus Christ given by his disciples like my friend Paul Empie. It is thus with great personal esteem and affection for him that I have welcomed the opportunity to write this brief foreword to his book.

Paul Empie devoted his life to the service of our Lord. His faith in Jesus Christ led him to recognize the Lord in those in need aided by the relief services of the Lutheran World Federation. Yet, precisely because his charity was an expression of his faith and not mere good works, Paul Empie was deeply concerned about the scandal of disunity between followers of the one Lord, reborn through the one baptism, worshiping the one God and Father of all. He always saw our dialogues not merely as an academic exercise, but as a service to the faithful of our churches. That is why he insisted that theologians think not only about their own fields of specialization, but also about the faith of the Christian people and their reconciliation through the blood of Christ.

Paul Empie has now entered eternity. He has appeared before the Risen and Triumphant Savior. In the fullness of the Lord's kingdom there are no more divisions. I pray that all Christians who have joined this assembly of witnesses (cf. Hebrews 12:1) will support with their prayers before the Lamb (cf. Revelation 8:3–4) the work of those who make theirs the prayer of our common Lord: that here on earth all may be one in Him, to the glory of God (cf. John 17:21).

Praised be Jesus Christ.

William Cardinal Baum

Rome, October 15, 1980

EDITOR'S PREFACE

How quickly time passes. On July 6, 1965, representatives of Roman Catholic and Lutheran churches met to open dialogues between the churches. The talks were to be so deliberate they would take ten years. But the ten years were soon gone and the talks over. The results of the meetings were compressed into reports and left to the fate of time, library shelves, and would-be readers. Readers there have been, and endurance there has been. The reports have been proving themselves worthy of time.

To open the reports to a wider audience, they have now been condensed into this study book and explained in a popular style by one of the chairpersons of the dialogues, Paul C. Empie.

The reports were not easy to explain. As the dialogues progressed, they became more and more technical. The report on the first dialogue was thirty-six pages long. The report on the last was 368 pages long—and in fine print. The intensification was probably a good sign, but it made difficult work for a writer of a book like this because the discussions became so intricate. Readers of this study book will find that the first chapters are easy going, but the last chapters are a good theological workout. Even if the ideas cannot be completely understood, however, readers can get a glimpse of how a dialogue unfolds and how teachings are thought through in detail.

The reports and explanations will be most lively if readers will engage in miniature dialogues of their own. Arrangements can be made with other Lutherans and Catholics to meet to discuss the dialogues. Suggestions for planning the sessions are found at the end of the Introduction, and further suggestions for the discussions are found at the end of each chapter. Seven sessions would be needed to cover the material well.

How quickly lives pass. On that same July 6, 1965, the dialogues opened with participants who were active, leading thinkers of the churches. Today, several of them are no longer living—T. Austin Murphy, John Courtney Murray, Arthur Carl Piepkorn, Warren Quanbeck, Kent S. Knutson, and the author of this study book himself, Paul C. Empie. They gave us their thoughts as part of their last work. Their papers can be read in full in the dialogue reports which follow. Dr. Empie's explanations have become his memoirs.

The dialogues have passed, lives have passed, an era has passed; but here and there Christians converse and a momentum continues. This study guide is given us to serve that process.

THE REPORT DOCUMENTS

Lutherans and Catholics in Dialogue I–III, Paul C. Empie and T. Austin Murphy, eds. (Minneapolis: Augsburg Publishing House): I—"The Status of the Nicene Creed as Dogma of the Church"; II—"One Baptism for the Remission of Sins"; III—"The Eucharist as Sacrifice."

Lutherans and Catholics in Dialogue IV: Eucharist and Ministry, Paul C. Empie, T. Austin Murphy, eds. (New York, Washington, D.C.: Jointly published by U.S.A. National Committee of the Lutheran World Federation and the Bishops' Commission for Ecumenical Affairs, 1970).

Lutherans and Catholics in Dialogue V: Papal Primacy and the Universal Church, Paul C. Empie and T. Austin Murphy, eds. (Minneapolis: Augsburg, 1974).

Lutherans and Catholics in Dialogue VI: Teaching Authority and Infallibility in the Church, Paul C. Empie, T. Austin Murphy, and Joseph A. Burgess, eds. (Minneapolis: Augsburg, 1980).

The following are the original publications which were reprinted under one cover in the first title listed on the previous page. The citations in the text refer to the following originals:

The Status of the Nicene Creed as Dogma of the Church (New York, Washington, D.C.: Jointly published by U.S.A. National Committee of the Lutheran World Federation and the Bishops' Commission for Ecumenical Affairs, 1965).

Lutherans and Catholics in Dialogue II: One Baptism for the Remission of Sins, Paul C. Empie and William W. Baum, eds. (New York, Washington, D.C.: Jointly published by U.S.A. National Committee of the Lutheran World Federation and the Bishops' Commission for Ecumenical Affairs, 1966).

Lutherans and Catholics in Dialogue III: The Eucharist as Sacrifice, Paul C. Empie and T. Austin Murphy, eds. (New York, Washington, D.C.: Jointly published by U.S.A. National Committee of the Lutheran World Federation and the Bishops' Commission for Ecumenical Affairs, 1967).

INTRODUCTION

The Barriers of Prejudice

Prejudices run deep. Inherited prejudices run deeper. Four centuries of ill will between Lutheran and Catholic individuals and groups have created emotional as well as social and political barriers. Yet all of us have claimed the same Christ as our Lord and Savior.

My own ancestors came to this country in 1708 fleeing religious persecution, and persecution is not easy to forget! The early twentieth-century American society in which I was reared knew all about the more deplorable aspects of "Romish Rule" and the horrors of the Spanish Inquisition, with the result that any local instance of growth in Roman Catholic political power was viewed with much distrust. Little was said about the instances when Protestants had dealt cruelly with Roman Catholics.

In our own time, resistance to antiabortion laws and to public tax support for parochial schools has been motivated to a considerable degree by the same fear of Roman Catholic domination. Rigid views of separation of church and state have resulted.

When we view each other in caricature, we substitute labels for people, and the consequence is dehumanizing to both parties. Fear not only imagines barriers; it creates them. Roman Catholics and Protestants alike have indulged the practice of comparing themselves at their best with others at their worst. This is both dishonest and stupid, fraudulent and reprehensible. It makes us victims of pride and hate. Truth goes unnoticed and dies unmourned. Praiseworthy service to humanity is discounted and explained away as the ulterior product of less significant sins. All of us have been guilty of these biases and their ills.

For Example

This mutual disparagement is seen in two illustrations. I was chairperson of Lutheran Church Productions Incorporated, the agency which produced the film *Martin Luther.* Shortly after its release, someone sent me a clipping from the bulletin of a Roman Catholic parish in South Carolina. Its priest had written something like this: "I hear that some Catholics are worried because the Lutherans have a film about Martin Luther. That doesn't bother me a bit! They have every right to produce a film about their founder. What we Catholics should do is produce a film about our founder—Jesus Christ!"

That was a cheap shot, but less vulgar than the Protestant yarn about the priest needling an Irish parishioner about his Italian foreman. "How do you like your dago boss, Pat?" he inquired. "Fine, Father; how do you like yours?" Pat shot back. This joke added religious prejudice to ethnic prejudice. I heard it in a meeting of my church council, where presumably we had come together to serve the interests of Christ's whole Body. I report it with shame. Such deep-rooted emotional prejudices continue to exist, but fortunately evidences of Christian love and understanding have been appearing to offset them.

I could cite many more illustrations of the ill will of the centuries.

Changes in the Climate

Suddenly on March 4, 1974, the *New York Times* carried a front page story telling the public that Lutherans and Catholics have reached "accord" on papal primacy (a considerable overstatement, as we shall detail later). Many Lutherans were stunned. They had known in a vague way that theological conversations were going on with Roman Catholic theologians, but this was going too far! One irate lady wrote in a letter to *The Lutheran,* "I am outraged to learn that some Lutheran theologians are advocating Lutheran acceptance of the papacy even in a limited capacity. There is no compromise . . . . In their anxiety for unity these theologians may exchange acceptance of the papacy for empty pews in Lutheran churches."

What happened? A lot, mostly quietly and unprogrammed (unless as some of us think, by the Holy Spirit). This context is important; a few elements should be mentioned here. (A very readable account of this background is given by Warren A. Quanbeck in his excellent book *Search for Understanding: Lutheran Conversations with Reformed, Anglican, and Roman Catholic Churches.* I shall refer to his book again; it is worthwhile reading for anyone who wishes a broader perspective on ecumenical dialogues.)

Getting to Know You . . .

Mutual discovery has contributed a great deal to the progress of the dialogues. The discovery has occurred in a variety of ways.

I recall talking to pastors in Germany after World War II who had collaborated with the underground resistance against the Nazis, and had encountered Roman Catholic priests doing the same thing. "I recognized the integrity of their Christian faith and learned to love them as brothers," one pastor told me, and added, "I shall never allow prejudice to separate us again."

Many of us experienced the same feeling in the course of cooperation with Roman Catholic agencies in resettlement and relief programs, both domestic and overseas. Mutual respect, trust, and appreciation were the rule, not the exception. I saw this cooperation on a memorable visit to eastern Tanzania. The Lutheran World Federation was able to send aid to refugees there from the Congo (now Zaire) only because the Catholic White Fathers had established a border mission which distributed the supplies on our behalf. The bishop was host to Mrs. Empie and myself. We stayed overnight at the mission and were deeply impressed by the work they were doing, and grateful that they were there to do it.

Many instances of fruitful partnership could be cited, especially in the fields of race, justice, and human rights. These occasions involved thousands of persons who discovered each other in the process.

The Effect of Biblical and Historical Research

In recent decades, Roman Catholics have become more intensely engaged in biblical studies. This has had a notable theological consequence because it has led to considerable contact and sharing between members of the seminary faculties of the two traditions. The Lutheran and Roman Catholic professors found little disagreement in the field of biblical scholarship. As lectureships were exchanged, the participants discovered that many of the deadlocks of the Reformation period had lost their force. Sharp differences had been softened by changing circumstances, discovery of new data, clarifications of terminology, or in some cases, by the shifts of emphases which had taken place.

This was brought to my attention dramatically at Baltimore in March 1965 when Lutheran and Roman Catholic representatives first met to plan dialogues. As we decided on topics for discussion and drew up ground rules, each group met separately to compile its list of proposals. When we reassembled and compared lists, I was astonished to find that neither list included the subject of "Scripture versus Tradition" or of "Justification by Grace Through Faith." When I inquired about the omissions, I was told that the theologians, and even the church authorities, were no longer disagreeing on these subjects sufficiently to warrant special sessions to debate them! That may have been a bit optimistic (as we shall also see later); but I responded that, if that development were true, it was so important that we needed to let the churches know about it! No longer could we let the churches assume that all of the divisive issues of the sixteenth century still separated Lutherans from Roman Catholics. Many of the differences had simply disappeared!

The Role of Vatican II

History came together at the Second Vatican Council (1962–64). There positions converged and climates changed. The council found a new approach to the ministry of the people of God. It opened up new perspectives, brought fresh insights, and afforded opportunities for broader interpretations of conciliar and papal teachings. And it did all of this without repudiating long-standing dogmas or doctrinal decisions. The council did much for relations with the Christian communions outside of the Roman Catholic Church by acknowledging them. It used the term *ecclesial reality,* an undefined description. That healed many old wounds.

Vatican II, in fact, was the signal which led us in the U.S.A. National Committee of the Lutheran World Federation to seek conversations with Roman Catholic theologians in this country. We had just completed a fruitful round of talks with representatives of the Reformed and Presbyterian traditions and felt that the time might be ripe to undertake discussions with an appropriate group within the Roman Catholic Church.

Fortunately—one could say providentially—the National Conference of Catholic Bishops in the U.S.A. at that very time established a standing Commission on Ecumenical Affairs. The Commission's first executive was Monsignor William Baum (subsequently the Cardinal-Archbishop of the Diocese of Washington). I contacted him on his first day in office and together we began to work out the procedures for the dialogues.

Purposes and Hopes

"Why these dialogues?" we are often asked. "What are your motives, your goals? What do you hope to achieve by them?"

In a sense, the primary motive may be that of the compulsion to demonstrate *integrity.* Scripture makes plain that the church is *one:* Christ prayed that his followers might be one as he and the Father were one, and St. Paul speaks of the church as the Body of Christ. Every Christian claims to belong to that Body; not to just a part of it, but to its totality. Indeed, if I do not belong to *all* of that Body, I don't belong to *any* of it! There is no such thing as being incorporated in a part separate from the whole. Thus, if I am not concerned about unity in the church and the well-being of all its parts, I am deficient in my understanding of the Christian faith. Specifically, I must be as much concerned about the Roman Catholics in Christ's Body, as I am about the Lutherans in it; I cannot turn my back on the Catholics without snubbing the Christ who dwells within them. For a Christian of any integrity, the pursuit of unity is not an optional matter.

Furthering Christian Mission

The fragmentation of the church handicaps its mission and often belies its witness to the gospel. When considering this point one must distinguish between (1) visible unity in functions such as intercommunion or mutual recognition of ministries and (2) visible unity through structures such as actual merger of the churches. If the latter could be achieved while protecting Christian freedom, stimulating and nurturing special insights, and fostering a rich dynamic pluralism within authentic apostolic teachings, it should not be ruled out as an ultimate goal. But the former is indispensable to faithful discipleship. Separate structures do not of necessity betray the authenticity of the gospel witness, but quarrelsome relationships between Christians do! It was Dr. Roswell P. Barnes, at that time Associate General Secretary of the National Council of Churches, who opened my eyes to this truth. "No single tradition can claim to have mined exhaustively the riches of God's revelation," he said to me. "Separate structures can live and work together in love, each serving the other and the whole in special and unique ways. The scandal of Christian disunity is instead *contentiousness,* the claim of any group to be the sole possessor of truth, to have an exclusive line to the Holy Spirit and the right (or duty) to exclude all others from fellowship. The pride and arrogance of this kind of sectarianism betrays the Gospel."

Thus if I care at all about the church's mission, I must do all I can to remove those things which undermine it. Disunity in the sense of contentiousness, fragmentation of Christian fellowship, and absence of mutual serving love, cripples my witness to the gospel.

Christian Interdependence

A third motivation is our need of each other: to help us deepen our spiritual strength and insight. This is not so much a need to huddle together as the world runs against Christian ideals and hopes, though that motivation should not be overlooked. Growth in church membership is not keeping up with the growth in world population. At the end of every day, Christians become a slightly smaller minority among the peoples of the earth. The Christian voice is disregarded by more and more people.

But the size of the church has never affected the vitality of the Christian witness. It's the other way around! Relationships, not numbers, count. People grow in the interaction of relationships, and Christians attain their full stature only in the whole Body of which Christ is the Head. No part of the body can function adequately in isolation. I am convinced that the Lutheran tradition has preserved and transmitted an authentic understanding of the apostolic faith, and I cherish it. Yet I gratefully acknowledge that every time I have gone to these dialogue meetings with Roman Catholic brethren, I have learned something new. My faith has been enriched with added insights. At the same time, not only have I gained a widened circle of comrades in Christ whose personal friendship is precious, but I have also become conscious of my shared identity in the Lord's Body with the entire Roman Catholic communion. This has come about in a real way, not just an academic way.

The result of these associations has been an upsurge in spirit, accompanied by joy and gratitude to God. I have noted the same signs in other group members on both sides. Without the gifts we have shared with each other, we would all be poorer. I repeat, we *need* this direct relationship within the church in order to be the Lord's Body and to deepen the understanding and experience of the grace of God. Once this is recognized and the parts grow as they function together under the Head, structures will begin to take care of themselves.

Objectives of the Dialogue

Having touched upon the why, let's take a look at the what of the dialogues. Precisely what are we trying to do? Some of the goals are short-range, while others are of necessity long-range. The latter may seem less attainable than the former, but here again the working of the Holy Spirit may surprise human calculations.

Getting the Facts

One of our objectives has been described by a participant as clearing out the theological underbrush which obstructs the path to fellowship. The theological tangles of the Reformation period entrapped the followers down through the centuries until each party felt obligated to cling to its position. Today, however, there are Roman Catholic scholars who assert that the Council of Trent, which condemned Luther's teachings in wholesale fashion, actually did not understand precisely what Luther taught. Communications in that day were not all that good, and those who opposed him for a variety of reasons—not all theological—had the louder voices. On the other side, Lutherans who at first were objecting to what they regarded as abuses in the preaching and practices of the church began to regard these deviations as the norms by which the entire Roman Catholic Church and its doctrines should be judged and found wanting. Major differences in doctrinal understandings and emphases, which did indeed develop, monopolized attention; while the much larger areas of agreement in the apostolic faith were increasingly ignored.

Quite apart from taking sides in the sixteenth-century skirmishes, one should ask: To what extent do these real or alleged doctrinal differences of that time still exist in the contemporary teachings of Lutherans and Roman Catholics? The dialogues demonstrated conclusively that even the participants were not completely informed about each other's current positions. While competent theologians had a general grasp of the current situation, the dialogue sessions (which occurred over more than a decade) exposed the lack of mutual information. In spite of my own frequent contacts with Roman Catholic representatives at the national and international levels, my superficial impressions of the teachings and practices of their church were embarrassing!

Some Misconceptions

This lack of up-to-date information permits the deep-seated prejudices and inhibitions to continue to handicap us. No one is completely free from these encumbrances. For example, Lutherans have labeled Roman Catholics as "Virgin Mary worshipers," or have dismissed them as people who know little and care less about the Bible. Both allegations are false. Word of that misconception hasn't gotten around.

From the other side, some Roman Catholics assume that Lutherans have abandoned most Christian teachings because the Lutherans reject the universal authority of the bishop of Rome. I was told of a "cottage dialogue" in Montclair, New Jersey, at which a Roman Catholic participant was astonished to learn that Protestants believed in the deity of Jesus Christ! That Lutherans teach the "real" presence of Christ in the Sacrament of Holy Communion came as a complete surprise. These caricatures of each other must be exposed for what they are.

Problems of Language

Clearing up misunderstanding is only part of the process. Clear communication is required if genuine empathy and fellowship is to be achieved. This realization hit us all in our very first encounter at Baltimore. The problem came in the way we used words. We had different meanings for the same words! At each crucial point we had to ask: What meaning is being conveyed by the words which are used? How might it be stated in other words? What would be an opposite meaning? We quickly found that we had indeed been talking about different things in our respective traditions, though we had used the same words. More about this in the chapter dealing with the Nicene Creed.

The Question of Objectivity

To understand another person in the meaning which that person intends his or her statement to convey is no simple matter. Certainly in the field of religious thought and insight, there is no such thing as complete, detached objectivity. Involved is the problem of epistemology, how we get to know or believe something. Whether or not I like it or admit it, I am a product of my past. All my life I have been influenced by parents, teachers, and other forceful personalities who have helped to shape the person I have become. My patterns of thought are thereby affected. I have certain deep-seated emotional biases. Instinctive reactions are developed and conditioned by past experience. My viewpoint is shaped by the presuppositions I bring to each problem. None of my judgments is entirely free from the values I hold, incoherent or inconsistent as they may be at times. How can anybody understand so complex a person? Even those closest to me are only partially successful.

In one of our dialogue sessions, we were discussing the role of the Virgin Mary in Christian faith. One of the Roman Catholic participants exclaimed, "The biblical account and the honor accorded to her in the early church is important and interesting, but not decisive for me. The veneration of Mary is a meaningful part in my devotional life, and no research is going to take it away from me." A Lutheran may not share that experience, but he or she must learn to understand it free from prejudice or condescension. Indeed one must have the courage and honesty to recognize that most persons espouse the viewpoint of the traditions in which they were raised and nurtured, though those viewpoints are different, and though the persons are of equal intelligence, integrity, and religious sophistication. If there is more than a small measure of truth in this fact, is not the goal of understanding hopeless? But perfection is not our goal. What we seek is movement toward greater integrity and unity in the Body of Christ. In that context, each step toward greater understanding brings us closer toward the goal of unity in truth; meanwhile, love bridges the narrowing gaps.

For the Christian, that love is not academic, it comes alive in relationships. Thus I must stress the significance of the personal appreciation, trust, and affection engendered in the days spent in seeking out each other in Christ. How I regret that the prejudices of the past deprived me during most of my life of this enriching fellowship! I thank my Lord that this experience has drawn me deeper into the unity of His Body.

Honesty and Responsibility in Furthering Unity

But let's get down to earth. If we clear the underbrush of misinformation and caricatures and grow in understanding, will our separated lives come together again? Will not genuine differences keep us going our respective ways? That is what those dialogues were all about, and that is what we will be discussing in succeeding chapters. Some of us hoped at the beginning that sufficient agreement in the apostolic faith might be found to permit joint worship, including intercommunion. Although this has occurred occasionally in local situations, it does not yet have the blessing and sanction of church authorities. The necessary growth together in the faith has not as yet taken place everywhere.

We did decide early in our discussions that we should study the problem of intercommunion, and we did spend one meeting on it; but we quickly realized that we first had to discuss what valid ministries are and how they are recognized. Thus the question of intercommunion was postponed. Many of us still dare to hope, however, that intercommunion will be officially approved within a decade or two.

Beyond that hope lies the possibility of some formal structural ties. The chapter dealing with papal primacy looks at that option and makes some modest suggestions. Psychological obstacles loom enormous. They could hardly be overcome in our generation. Some persons have serious reservations that the legitimate variety of historic Christian traditions could ever be guaranteed by a monolithic structure. However the issue of papal primacy is resolved, there must be some provision to encourage fresh insights; to promote creative pluralism in authentic Christian faith; and to protect Christian freedom against the encroachment of bureaucracy which almost inevitably tends to stress uniformity at the expense of unity based on conviction.

One should not dismiss these and other objections lightly. Behind most of them in one way or another are some nagging questions: Are we selling out? Are we compromising truth for unity and ending up with something spurious? Are we betraying our spiritual forefathers who were willing to die "for the faith"? Did they lie to us when they taught us the central differences or why do they now tell us those differences were only marginal? Has anyone admitted error at one point or another? Has anyone otherwise changed positions? If mistakes could be made at the Reformation, how can we be sure others are not being made now?

When Is a Conviction a Conviction?

Answers to such questions as those noted above will be suggested in the succeeding chapters. A prior question should be mentioned here. It is this: Since honest dialogue involving any of my religious convictions must be entered into with an open mind, does not my willingness to question my conviction betray my conviction? Would not considering other options openmindedly undermine a conviction?

To look at an inexact analogy, if a husband considers the possibility of living with another woman, does not this very fact indicate that he does not really love his wife? Is not looking elsewhere already a betrayal? This is no straw-man issue, whether or not we like to admit it. Loyalties to the church and its traditions are not easily dislodged, even in the face of the most persuasive evidence.

A routine response is that a fearless faith fears no test. A confident faith welcomes a test. Reticence shows insecurity.

Another response is that the dialogues are not dealing with contradictions. When we dialogued with Marxists in a different encounter we were dealing with contradictions, but in the Christian tradition dialogists we were not. Lutherans and Roman Catholics alike belong to the Body of Christ, and any agreements which may differ from past positions will not change that status a bit. Thus the confrontation aspect of dialogue can be displaced by shared concentration in the common search for more complete truth.

Furthermore, I have been living with convictions all my life; but as I have grown and matured, they have grown with me, and even changed at points. To be human is to be fallible; to refuse to consider the possibility of error or change is to be arrogant or stupid—or both.

The Distinction Between Fact and Truth

The late Franklin Clark Fry spoke of the "twin imperatives of truth and unity." A Christian must not scuttle truth for the sake of unity, but neither dare he abandon unity for the sake of absolute truth. Commitment to both truth and unity is essential to the obedient witness of the church.

In this connection, a distinction between *truth* and *factuality* must be mentioned. Too often the terms are interchanged. When we say London is in England, that is a statement of factual truth. When we say we regard the deity of Jesus Christ, that is true. The former is a fact which can be outwardly verified and can stand by itself. My faith in Jesus as Lord and Savior cannot be verified in the same way. It is a conviction certified from above and within rather than from evidence observable by anyone. Just what I mean by this "truth" is always partial and incomplete, subject to ever new depths of insight and understanding. It seems to me that the truths that almost everyone lives by, fall into this category of faith—not provable logically, empirically or scientifically (which is not to say that they are necessarily irrational or illogical).

Linguistic analysis is not my field, and specialists may have other ways of stating the distinction I've made here; but the distinction must be made. Too often it is not. In a college philosophy class we once argued whether religion can be taught, or whether it must be caught. The answer is both, for while faith is never without content which generally is rooted in human experience and passed on from generation to generation, something within me must recognize it as true if it is to be actually *my* faith. Herein lies a major value of dialogue—to assess the genuineness of conviction. Many persons have had the content of faith spoon-fed to them in Sunday school or catechetical classes. They swallowed it without personal reflection and appropriation. Yes, convictions can and should be *tested,* despite the risks which accompany the process.

A Pilgrimage with Risks

The purpose of this book is to encourage as many members as possible in the parishes to test their faith with all the risks involved, in obedience to the twin imperatives of truth and unity. One may hope that local dialogues between Lutherans and Roman Catholics will be spawned in the process. It is a kind of pilgrimage which demands both time and effort, and may result in sore feet. Those undertaking it will soon find out that at one point or another virtually every basic tenet of their Christian faith will be touched upon and scrutinized. A major outcome should be the exhilaration of corporate growth in understanding and experiencing God's grace.

To do the job seriously, reference should be made to the reports entitled *Lutherans and Catholics in Dialogue*. They are not easy reading. Some essays are quite technical, written by theologians for theologians. Since all the conversations about them were off the record in order to encourage complete candor, the progress from the essays to the final summary statements cannot always be traced. The chapters of this book will try to offer some help at this point.

The Status of the Common Statements and Essays

Keep in mind that the essays and summary statements are *not* official positions of either church tradition. They are rather the opinions of the authors. Since the writers are highly competent and trusted theologians in their respective churches, their judgments should not be regarded lightly, for each took seriously his *representative* role in the dialogue. It is anticipated that eventually the churches will take official recognition of these documents and deal appropriately with their contents.

Needless to say, the statements in this book are the sole responsibility of the author. I have written in the first person to emphasize this fact. Since I have been at all the meetings, I report from the inside, so to speak.

During the earlier sessions, I had a standard speech which went something like this, "Since I am virtually the only person here who is not a professional theologian, I am a key participant. If what we are doing cannot be conveyed to the whole church, its fruits will be limited. You fellows are up on cloud seven with your technical theological language, while I have my feet at the parish level and speak that language. If I don't understand what you are saying, neither will those in the congregations. So please make it plain to me. (And that includes all your quotes and footnotes in Latin, Greek, and German!)"

Enough knotty problems have been raised in this introductory chapter to stimulate more discussion than time may permit. Among them are the following:

1. The matter of bias and prejudice. Do we recognize it in ourselves, and are we willing to struggle with it?
2. The scandal of disunity. Do we stereotype other churches and then make jokes about them?
3. The convergence of understandings. A growth together in understandings is better than an agreement to compromise. Compromises can betray.
4. The nature of wholeness. If we don't belong to the *whole* church, we don't belong to *any* part of it.
5. The nature of convictions. How can we maintain our convictions while keeping an open mind?
6. The relation of truth to unity. Commitment to truth requires commitment to unity and vice versa. A creative tension exists between the two.
7. The nature of truth. There is a difference between fact and faith.

Don't expect to get solutions to these problems quickly. I've been wrestling with them all my life.

DISCUSSION

Suggestions for an Introductory Discussion

This condensation of the Lutheran-Roman Catholic dialogues could be used in several ways:

- In neighborhood interfaith discussion groups
- In church school and parish study groups
- By ministerial groups
- As private reading

The purpose of the discussions would be to help participants clarify their own understanding of the faith and listen constructively to the understanding of others. Suggestions for discussion will be supplied with each section.

If an interfaith discussion is organized, the Lutheran participants might supply these discussion guides for half of the sessions, and the Roman Catholic participants could provide material supplied by their parish or church offices for the other half of the sessions.

The suggestions for the last session include a plan for exchange visits at the worship services of others who participate in the discussions. The visits could incorporate a discussion time after the services for questions about the worship forms. These visits could be interspersed through the sessions if the group prefers.

For the introductory discussion:

- On a chalkboard or newsprint write as six headings the subjects discussed in the dialogues. From left to right on the chalkboard they are Creed, Baptism, Eucharist, Ministers, Papal Primacy, and Teaching Authority. Items will be filled in under the headings as the session progresses.
- Have the participants recall instances in which they discovered how much the beliefs of their congregation had in common with those of other congregations and churches. As the participants do so, list the similarities under the most related heading on the chalkboard.
- Have the participants recall instances in which they noticed differences between other churches and their church. As they do so, list the differences under the related headings.
- Have the participants recall instances in which they were told how wrong the other church was. Have them especially recall charges which turned out to be untrue, prejudicial, and stereotypical.
- At the top left of the chalkboard write *unity* and at the top right write *truth.* Help the group see that the churches have more unity of agreement on creeds and Baptism and less on infallibility. The churches tend to differ on what is truth in matters of infallibility and teaching authority. To get acquainted, the discussions will begin with areas of agreement.
- As another learning, directly under *unity* write a belief the group would be willing to sacrifice to have unity. Then under *truth* write some belief group members might not want to give up to have unity. For example, the Christian church would not sacrifice its belief about Christ to have unity. (The churches already agree on the belief about Christ—stated in the creeds.) On the other hand, to have unity a church would surely give up its beliefs about what color should be placed on the altar on a certain day. What are some matters that are more contro-

versial which the churches might or might not want to give up just to have unity (for example, beliefs about church authority)? This grouping of ideas could help participants see the tension between truth and unity. They will see some beliefs which they would never sacrifice for unity, and some beliefs which might be sacrificed for unity because unity is an important belief itself. This illustrates the tension between truth and unity.

Have members of the group pick out some of the differences they identified earlier to see what they might consider giving up to have unity, and what they might want to retain to preserve what they believe to be truth. Then have them note the similarities they listed to see what unity already exists. How did the similarities come about? Could the differences be resolved in the same way?

CHAPTER 1

The Nicene Creed as Dogma in the Church

The term *dogma* is not normally used by Lutherans. They prefer the word *doctrine.* Yet their seminaries offer courses in dogmatics, and the term appears in the Lutheran Confessions, for example, in the *Formula of Concord* which states that the Scriptures are the only touchstone by which all dogmas must be judged. In Catholic usage, a doctrine usually explains a dogma and thus may be given less weight than the latter. A third category is that of theological opinion, which may be helpful for interpretation but has no binding character. The distinction between dogma and doctrine is often difficult to maintain, for at times the words are used interchangeably. In this book, the meaning of these two terms should be clear by the context within which they are used.

At the preliminary meeting of the dialogues in March 1965, the first question was: "How do we begin?" The answer came quickly. The first meetings should focus on *areas of agreement* rather than on areas of controversy. This procedure would afford opportunity for participants to get acquainted and to become accustomed to the terminology and ways of thinking characteristic of each tradition.

As we began listing areas of agreement, we immediately thought of the Nicene Creed. It is a series of dogmatic (doctrinal) statements held by both communions. The discussion of the Creed was to be followed by a discussion of Baptism—on which general agreement was also anticipated.

The start-with-agreements approach turned out to be wise and fruitful. Conversations became noticeably relaxed as names became fleshed out in personalities with dedicated minds and warm spirits.

Fewer sessions and preparatory documents were devoted to the Creed than to any of the other subjects discussed in the dialogues, but this should not be taken to mean that the Creed was dismissed as less significant. Indeed it was found to represent major agreements along with major challenges. Where there is agreement there is less to argue about and write about. Three study papers were prepared. Broad basic issues were uncovered and touched upon, and, as we shall see, some tough questions were asked.

The Role of Dogmatic Statements

"Why must we have creeds and dogmas?" one may ask. "Do not the Holy Scriptures provide all the information we need?" Some Christian groups are so sensitive on this point that they adopt such names as Bible Fellowship Church. They pay such exclusive attention to the Book that their critics sometimes accuse them of having a paper pope.

The answer to the question, "Why creeds?" lies in the fact that not all Christians interpret all parts of the Bible in the same way. Furthermore, their various understandings of the very nature of revelation in the Scriptures differ. That is one major reason why there are denominations in a divided church! All through its life the church has had to wrestle with differences of understanding. Some of the differences became so great they were labeled heresies. Many dogmas (but not all) were formulated in opposition to what was classified as heresy.

The summary statement in the dialogue report on the Creed says, "The Nicene Faith, formulated by the Council at Nicaea in 325 and developed in the Nicene-Constantinopolitan Creed, was a response to contemporary errors. The Church was obliged to state her faith in the Son in nonbiblical terms to answer the Arian question."

Arius, from whom the "Arian question" takes its name, said that Christ was created by the Father and thus is subordinate to him. It affects us all. At stake is the question "Who is Jesus Christ?"

As the summary statement points out: "The confession that Our Lord Jesus Christ is the Son, God of God, continues to assure us that we are in fact redeemed, for only He who is God can redeem us" (page 32). The words in the Nicene Creed, which Lutherans, like Roman Catholics, normally confess when they celebrate Holy Communion are, "the only Son of God, eternally begotten of the Father, God from God, Light from Light, True God from True God, begotten, not made, of one Being with the Father." These words are intended to clarify the person of Christ. In the paper John Courtney Murray prepared for the dialogues, he quoted the ancient Athanasian rule of faith given in a letter about the middle of the fourth century regarding the intention of the Council at Nicaea. "Thus, given that they (Father and Son) are one, and given that the divinity itself is one, the same things are said (in the Scripture) about the Son that are also said about the Father, except that the Son is not said to be Father" (page 18).

The Testimony of the Lutheran Confessions

The Lutheran Confessions (statements of belief) are detailed and explicit on the person of Christ. Article VIII of the *Formula of Concord* says:

> It is also taught among us that God the Son became man, born of the virgin Mary, and that the two natures, divine and human, are so inseparably united in one person that there is one Christ, true God and true man, who was truly born, suffered, was crucified, died.

The role of a creed is to formulate dogmas *to interpret the gospel* and *to protect the faith from error.* Dr. Warren Quanbeck notes that the Creeds are addressed to the needs of particular moments in history. This function is noted in his paper prepared for the dialogues. He cites two other functions as important: (1) The doxological use, that is, use in worship. (Doxology has to do with expressing the glory of *doxa,* of God, in praise.) (2) The self-identification use, that is, knowing who we are and what we stand for in a world filled with so many groups and beliefs. In his paper, Dr. Quanbeck characterizes these roles as follows:

> "Confession of the Nicene Creed is therefore first of all assertion of faith in God, of participation in the life offered in Christ, of obedience to the Spirit who reigns as Lord in the church . . .
>
> "Confession of the Nicene Creed is also one of the ways in which the Lutheran church seeks to make

known her self understanding. The ecclesiastical and theological disputes of the sixteenth century saw labels distributed generously. In this atmosphere the Lutheran church seeks to identify herself as a church participating in the catholic tradition of the west, as standing in continuity with the one, holy, catholic and apostolic church . . ." (page 8).

This all seems quite simple. If Lutherans and Roman Catholics both consider the dogmas in the Nicene Creed as binding, and share these views of its role, what did the theologians talk about for two whole days? They talked about the underlying issues, and they found those so complex that time ran out. Some of the issues had to be rescheduled for discussion in connection with topics on the agenda for later sessions.

Are Dogmas Revelation?

A question which comes up early is whether the Creeds are revealed the same as Scripture is revealed. The joint statement made by the dialogue participants asserts that the Nicene faith is "grounded in the biblical proclamation about Christ and the trinitarian baptismal formulas used in the Church." The key word is "grounded."

I recall that during the discussion, the question was raised why the Creed did not use biblical language to express the faith. The answer given was that the heresies which were refuted by the Creeds used nonbiblical language, and they therefore had to be answered in their own terms; but that did not mean that the Creeds were nonbiblical in substance. All of the Nicene doctrines were rooted in Scripture. Between Scripture and dogma there is an identity of sense. The dogma has the "mind" of the Scriptures, the answer asserted. But a New Testament scholar retorted, "Nonsense, the Nicene Creed has things in it which the writers of Scripture never even thought of!" I would surmise that he was referring to such concepts as "being of one substance with the Father," and "who proceedeth from the Father and the Son."

Murray deals with this problem in his paper. He minces no words. He says the teachings of the church are as true for the faith as the Scriptures. He quotes Pope Pius XII: ". . . the truths which are taught by the living magistery (official teaching authority) are contained in Sacred Scripture and *in the divine tradition, be it implicitly or explicitly* . . . God has given to his Church the living magistery, in order that the truths which are contained in the deposit of faith only obscurely and in some implicit fashion may be brought to light and formulated. The divine Redeemer entrusted this deposit to the magistery of the Church alone, not to the individual Christian or even to theologians" (pages 16–17, emphasis and parentheses added).

Murray pursues this point to its logical conclusion: "It is evident that the Nicene Church considered the relationship between the Scriptures and the magistery to be reciprocal. The word of God in the Scriptures was regarded as the norm of the faith of the Church . . . . At the same time, the Nicene Church considered it to be the magisterial function of the Church to interpret the Scriptures and to declare their sense in formulas that were to be accepted by faith on pain of exclusion from the communion of the faithful. The word of God, therefore, is the norm for the magistery in declaring the faith of the Church. At the same time, the magisterial interpretation of the word of God and its declaration in the word of the Church is normative of the faith of the Church" (pages 18–19).

In other words, because dogmas (that is, the affirmations of the Nicene Creed) are derived from the explicit or implicit teachings of Scripture and from the "divine tradition" declared by the teaching authorities of the church, they are certified as true Christian faith. This puts them on a par with revelation.

Differences and Similarities

Probably most, if not all, Lutherans squirm when they hear this reasoning, especially when Pius XII places "the divine tradition" alongside of Sacred Scripture and thereby gives it equal billing. The joint summary statement points this out by saying, "The way in which doctrine is certified as dogma is not identical in the two communities, for there is a difference in the way in which mutually acknowledged doctrine receives ecclesiastical sanction."

I believe, however, that the Lutherans are as much like the Catholics on dogma as they are different. In his paper Dr. Warren Quanbeck has this to say about the Scriptures: ". . . the Word of God . . . calls the church into being, maintains and preserves her, and the church lives in loyalty and obedience to this Word. The prophetic and apostolic witness to Jesus Christ the Word of God is found in the Scriptures, which for this reason have a primary place in the church. The authority of Scripture is the authority of the Word of God, that is, the authority of the God who speaks in and through them. This authority must not be understood in a literalistic, legalistic, or atomistic way, but is to be seen in the light of three factors. 1. The Holy Spirit . . . . It is the work of the Holy Spirit which enables men to hear God's voice in the Scriptures. 2. The Ministry. God has bestowed the gift of ministry upon His church. It accomplishes its task of serving God and men through the proclamation of the gospel. God uses this proclamation in sermon, sacrament, teaching, counseling and service to effect His saving presence among His people. 3. The Problem of Interpretation. The Scriptures require interpretation, a task which has literary, historical and theological dimensions. The interpreter is concerned to discover what the biblical writer intended to communicate to his readers, and for this work he avails himself of the lexical, literary and historical information which illuminate the text in its historical setting . . ." (pages 6–7). So Scriptures require interpretation, which may be a kind of tradition.

This too could cause some (but not most) Lutherans to squirm. The rift in the Lutheran Church—Missouri Synod in the middle 1970s hinged on this problem. One will note that in Quanbeck's statement, Scripture and the Word of God are not said to be identical. Over fifty years ago, Dr. Charles M. Jacobs gave an inaugural address at the Lutheran Theological Seminary at Philadelphia which contained the affirmation: "We do not identify (the Scriptures) with the Word of God," followed by the statement that the Bible "passes down from generation to generation the record of God's Word." He was roundly denounced by a wide range of Lutheran theologians and churches at that time. I dare say that a lot of Lutherans, clergy and lay, have not completely clarified their thinking on this point. If all parts of the Bible are not equally the Word of God, where is the line to be drawn and who does the drawing?

The Question of Authority

The question of authority is taken up again in Chapter 6. I should point out here, however, that Lutherans should side with Murray when he is unwilling to "make biblical scholarship the norm of the faith of the Church." He recalls that Arius quoted Scripture in support of his heresy; someone has to sort out biblical statements which seem in conflict. For example, Arius would give preeminence to John 14:28 ("for the Father is greater than I") over John 10:30 ("I and the Father are one"). The Council at Nicaea, acting as a teaching authority of the church at that time, reversed this order, not strictly on the basis of "biblical scholarship" but rather, in the words of George Lindbeck, "The Arian use of the NT . . . was heretical because it was, so to speak, opposed to the intention of the NT usage which was to exalt Christ, rather than to lower Him" (page 14).

There are as many varieties of biblical scholarship as there are Christian traditions. Luther felt that the doctrine of "justification by grace through faith" was the key to the right understanding of the Scriptures. A contemporary Lutheran theologian has described the Lutheran stance as one which sees Christ as the center of the scriptural witness, other parts being less important in proportion to their distance in significance from that center. Neither of these, nor any other, principle of scriptural interpretation is found explicitly in the Bible.

On what basis then do Lutherans believe their stance to be right? First, because they say faith in Christ should take priority over belief about the Bible, but also presumably because they are convinced that the Holy Spirit guided their forefathers and also sustains them in their convictions today. I surmise that Roman Catholics would say the same thing about their acceptance of their doctrines, that is, that they witness to the centrality of Christ and the influence of the Holy Spirit.

Similarities in Procedures

So although we act through different ecclesiastical tribunals and we come out with different results, the *process* of certification of Christian dogma seems strikingly similar. Lutherans, of course, concede that the teachings of their historic confessions are always subject to Scripture; but they often overlook the fact that they mean *their understanding* of Scripture, for no complete *common* understanding of it is to be found. No doubt Roman Catholics would say substantially the same thing, though in a different way. That Roman Catholic teaching should be contrary to Scripture is unthinkable for them. The point is that the church, guided by the Holy Spirit, develops explicitly what is implicit in Scripture. Where Scripture is silent, the church teaches authoritatively consistent with Scripture. But Scripture is primary to both.

I recall a report given at the National Lutheran Council after which it was said that more rabbits had been scared out than could be shot at! Maybe that's what dialogue is all about—to get the rabbits out into the open so at least we know they are there, whether we can deal with all of them immediately or not. From that point on, the analogy of shooting breaks down. We'll be more or less chasing out rabbits during the rest of this study, whether we can come to a conclusion about all of them or not. The purpose is to relieve suspicions about hidden viewpoints.

The Problem of the Development of Doctrine

How is doctrine developed? The final paragraph of the joint summary statement reads, "We together acknowledge that the problem of the development of doctrine is crucial today and is in the forefront of our common concern." Here is an issue just as difficult as the one about the relation between dogma and Scripture. It involves both the question of whether dogmas may ever be changed, and how dogmas are to be accepted by the Christian believer.

First, can dogma be changed? Lindbeck, in his somewhat technical but provocative paper lays the issue on the line in this way: ". . . the Catholic accepts the dogma as *irreformable* and the Protestant accepts the dogma as *reformable* in principle, at least" (page 12, emphases added). Both positions create problems not easily overcome.

Murray says that though we are certain of something, we may still grow to a fuller understanding within that certainty. He speaks of the "Immutability" of the Nicene dogma, and describes it as follows: "Immutability, like certainty, attaches to judgments, to affirmations, and to the sense in which the certain judgment or affirmation is made. On the other hand, the immutability of an affirmation, again like its certainty, does not preclude development—that is, fuller understanding—of the sense in which the affirmation is made.

"In the first place, therefore, it will be forever immutably true to say that the Son is consubstantial with the Father, that he is all that the Father is, except for the name of the Father. Moreover, it will be forever forbidden so to understand the

Nicene dogma—so to 'interpret' it, so to 'develop' its sense—as, in the end, to affirm that the Son is not consubstantial with the Father, not all that the Father is, except for the name of the Father. Finally, it will be forever forbidden to say that the Nicene dogma is mutable in the sense that it has or may become irrelevant, of no religious value or interest, no longer intelligible *suo modo* (in its own manner) as a formula of faith" (pages 21-22, parentheses added).

Dogmas and Doctrines

As I recall the discussion on this point, a distinction was made between (church) *dogma* and (theological) *doctrine* in Roman Catholic usage which helps in understanding their teaching of the development of doctrine. A *dogma* may be described as a tenet or concept in the Christian faith rooted in divine revelation and certified by the church as binding upon its members. A *doctrine* on the other hand, is an attempt to interpret the dogma more explicitly as it is enriched by the development in human understanding led by the Holy Spirit. The doctrines may expand, deepen, or perhaps even modify the dogma; but they may never reverse its basic proposition. In other words, no doctrine about the divinity of Christ may state that he is *not* divine! But there may be many ways, humanly speaking, of attempting to explain his divinity. With this distinction, doctrines do not have the same binding character as dogmas, having more the character of human and, thus, fallible efforts to explain divine mysteries.

This makes a lot of sense to me, though admittedly it raises the question of whether the Holy Spirit has less influence on doctrines than on dogmas. Obviously the central tenets of the Christian faith canot be reversed, for what would remain thereafter could no longer be called Christianity.

At this point, then, the conversation is saying that dogma cannot be changed, but a changed understanding of them can be developed in the doctrine in that the changed understanding is a fuller understanding of them. However, Lindbeck seemed to say that Protestants believe that the dogma itself can be changed. He said it is "reversible." Yet, presumably, Lindbeck would not consider the dogma of the deity of Christ "reversible." So what would be the implication of his statement that dogma is, "in principle, reformable"? There are two aspects of this problem, and both are very important.

Reformulating Versus Reversing

The joint summary statement declares that "The Nicene Faith possesses a unique status in the hierarchy of dogmas by reason of its testimony to and celebration of the mystery of the Trinity as revealed in Christ Our Savior . . ." (page 32). Notice the word *hierarchy*. It means the various levels of importance given to the various teachings. This hierarchy of dogmas and truths was frequently referred to in the dialogue discussions. The clear implication is that some dogmas are higher or more important than others. Lindbeck's question is precisely to this point: "Do the ancient Catholic symbols (Nicene Creed, for example) have in some sense a higher status than other dogmas of the church? If so, how can this be given effective expression in view of the fact that all dogmas are said (by many Roman Catholics) to be equally binding?" (page 11, parentheses added). What are contrasted here are the ecumenical Creeds—Apostles', Nicene, and Athanasian—and, for example, the recent dogmas about the Virgin Mary or papal infallibility. Lutherans have affirmed that these latter dogmas not only can but should be reversed, with no loss to the apostolic faith. For the Roman Catholic, as I understand it, the possibility exists of reformulation or reinterpretation—but not of reversal. Here we continue to differ.

But Lutherans are not off the hook. Granted that all church dogmas and doctrines are *in principle* reversible (because the scriptural witness to Christ stands above them), Lutherans do not *in practice* regard all of them as such. They do not expect that it will ever be permissible to deny the unity of the Son with the Father, as affirmed at Nicaea, or justification by grace alone through faith, as affirmed by the Reformers. Yet there are other dogmas and doctrines which they do regard as reversible (and may in fact wish to reverse). This creates a problem, for Lutherans do not have categories of dogma which are binding, as contrasted with categories of doctrine which are flexible. We have some unfinished homework here, as is attested by the intra-Lutheran tensions over the past generations which continue to some extent today.

A Hierarchy of Truths for Lutherans?

In the *Approved Constitution for Congregations of the Lutheran Church in America,* the Confession of Faith lists these elements in the following order:

- -Jesus Christ as Lord of the Church
- -The Gospel as the revelation of God's sovereign will and saving grace in Jesus Christ
- -The Holy Scriptures, the divinely inspired record of God's redemptive act in Christ, the norm for the faith and life of the church
- -The Apostles', Nicene, and Athanasian Creeds as true declarations of the faith of the Church
- -The Unaltered Augsburg Confession and Luther's Small Catechism as true witnesses to the Gospel
- -The other symbolical books—the Apology of the Augsburg Confession, the Smalcald Articles, Luther's Large Catechism, the Formula of Concord—as further valid interpretations of the confession of the church

Period! That's all. Not that this list doesn't represent a lot of pages of print, for it does that—an enormous amount of words, in fact. But obviously not all of it is dogma and doctrine, not even "the Holy Scriptures." Furthermore, there is a specific disclaimer with respect to dogmatic authority in the introduction to the *Formula of Concord,* which states, "Other writings, of ancient or modern teachers, whatever reputation they may have, should not be regarded as of equal authority with the Holy Scriptures, but should altogether be subordinated to them, and should not be received other or further than as witnesses, in what manner and at what places, since the time of the apostles, the doctrine of the prophets and apostles was preserved . . . the Holy Scriptures alone remain the only judge, rule, and standard, according to which, as the only touchstone, all dogmas should and must be judged, as to whether they be good or evil, right or wrong." A point of bitter dispute among Lutherans in past generations was whether the Confessions are accepted "insofar as" they agree with Scripture or "because" they agree with Scripture. Most would agree today that both apply since presumably all Christians would agree with the former; only Lutherans would affirm the latter.

The progression of thought in the Confession of Faith of the Lutheran Church in America—Christ, gospel, Scriptures, Creeds, confessions—seems to parallel, with respect to *norms,* the pattern earlier suggested as a Lutheran stance on *content*—

Christ as the center of a series of concentric circles of doctrines which diminish in proportion to their distance from the core. Obviously this notion rejects any fundamentalistic position that every line of Scripture is of equal importance. But the question arises, "What then does it mean to say that members of the Lutheran Church in America *accept* the three Creeds as 'true declarations' of the faith of the church, and the two groups of the historic Lutheran Confessions as 'true witnesses to the gospel' and further 'valid' interpretations of the confessions of the church?"

What Does the Word "Accept" Imply?

Thus, the problem of semantics rears its head again. This very issue was discussed at the Baltimore dialogue: Do Lutherans and Roman Catholics accept the Nicene Creed in the same sense? A hint of possible difference may be seen in a question raised in Lindbeck's paper. He had written that the words in the Nicene Creed "being of one substance with the Father" *(homoousion)* are immutable and cannot be developed or changed. Lindbeck asks:

"1. Granting that the 'came down from heaven' need not be understood as asserting anything erroneous, can a Roman Catholic nevertheless admit that its Gnostic overtones make it an unfortunate formulation (a) for us and/or, (b) even more seriously, in its original context?

"2. If the reply to '1' is to some degree affirmation, could similar doubts arise in reference to the *homoousion?* If not, why not?" (page 11).

This is difficult language for the nontheologian, but before we explain it, one more quote from Lindbeck: "Must one accept a metaphysical outlook according to which 'the dogmatic categories of being and substance' have priority over 'the scriptural categories of presence and function' with the result that it is possible to say that 'The Christian . . . now (after Nicaea) has come to understand more fully what Christ, the Lord with us, is'?" (page 15).

It is questionable whether the words used by the people of one era should become frozen and binding upon the people of a different era. The meanings of the words change. ("Came down from heaven" has a different meaning after moon shots and space explorations.)

I recall being somewhat taken aback during the discussion when a Roman Catholic participant stated that from one standpoint it was too bad that the Nicene Creed was ever written. He explained, "The Creed had to be formulated to protect the faith from heresies which had arisen. The danger lies in having the language which was used to refute the error become for all time the final and untouchable formulation in which the truth can be stated." Words used to refute heresies can become heresies themselves.

In order to affirm that Christ was not created by the Father, the Creed stated that he was "begotten, not made" and "of one being with the Father." These terms are largely foreign to modern thought-forms, and what they mean in a positive sense is difficult to explain. They are used to say Christ is *not* created because they are intending to make clear that he is not less than the Father. They serve this negative function adequately, but if one presses regarding the precise definition of divine "substance" or the word "begotten" in the positive sense, all sorts of images come to mind, and then one has to enter the realm of mystery where faith has to take over. Human language is inadequate.

Lindbeck's suggestion that some of these terms may have been unfortunate (though perhaps the best which could be found) and may even be misleading today, seems to be well taken.

Literal Images Versus Underlying Insights

Another facet of this problem can be illustrated by the following incident. A group of laypersons from a congregation near my home met regularly for Christian fellowship, including the discussion of faith concerns. Some of them had problems when reciting the Apostles' Creed in the worship service, specifically when they came to the statement "He descended into hell." (The basis for this *dogma* is a somewhat obscure and almost incidental reference in 1 Peter 3:19.) One person said flatly that the affirmation was meaningless to him, that he could make no sense of it, and that he remained silent at that point in the Creed. He felt that the image raised by the words was naive and incredible, and that to affirm belief in them was an act which lacked integrity. I was asked whether or not this attitude means one has no faith.

What did I say? I didn't beat around the bush. I replied that it did not invalidate one's Christian faith. Personally I don't hesitate to affirm that part of the Creed. Discounting the image evoked by both concepts, "descending" into hell and "ascending into heaven," neither of which have any literal (or spatial) meaning for me, they nevertheless evoke a profound sense of Christ's entering into the depths of human wretchedness and heights of divine exaltation. And I balance any skepticism with the stance expressed in the Lutheran confessions, "This article . . . cannot be comprehended with our senses and reasons, but must be apprehended by faith alone. Therefore it is our unanimous opinion that we should not engage in disputations concerning this article, but believe and teach it in all simplicity . . . . How this took place is something that we should postpone until the other world . . ." (*Formula of Concord,* Article IX).

Accept Versus Believe

To this I must add in all candor that I do not affirm this part of the Creed with the same conviction I bring to bear when I say that I "believe in God the Father Almighty" and "in Jesus Christ His only Son, our Lord." Perhaps the same word (believe) is not appropriate to both levels in this hierarchy of doctrines and truths. Believing in God has a different force from believing things about God. Is this an official Lutheran position? Not at all; it is my own, one Lutheran's; and I find it compatible with the Christ-centered and gospel-centered approach of the "Confession of Faith" of my church. It also says something about my understanding and use of Scripture.

An Analogy: The Liturgical and Doctrinal Use of the Psalms

Furthermore we should not overlook the two functions of the Creeds other than doctrinal as described by Quanbeck: self-identification and doxology (worship). In a sense the two blend in a single process. Use of the Creeds permits me to praise God—not *any* God, but the Father-Son-Holy Spirit to whom the Scriptures bear witness. By following from apostolic times, I *identify* myself with that *one, holy catholic, apostolic fellowship.* I confess my faith in the same God my spiritual ancestors were talking about, even if I may have some reservations about some of the language they used when speaking about him. Lindbeck points this out when he asks the question, "To what extent does the liturgical, 'doxological' character and use of these symbols give them special status? It is often said of dogmatic formulations that they are, in principle, capable of being improved upon. This, presumably, would never be said, for example, of the psalms. If they were mistakenly viewed as doctrinal definitions, they would obviously have to be regarded as deficient at many points in the light of the NT revelation; but it would appear that, even apart from the question of inspiration, their place in the liturgical heritage of the church makes it nonsensical to speak of 'improving' them. Could something analogous be said of the Catholic creeds?" (pages 11–12).

This arouses in my memory a session of the old Lutheran Ministerium of Pennsylvania years ago, when Psalm 139 was used in a devotional service. After the benediction, a pastor moved that if this psalm be used in the future, the closing verses be deleted. The verses said, "Do I not hate them that hate thee, O Lord? And do not I loathe them that rise up against thee? I hate them with a perfect hatred." The mover decried their content as contrary to the spirit of the New Testament revelation. He had a point—one could try to blunt the words by saying that the psalmist really meant that he hated the sin rather than the sinner, but I'd bet my bottom dollar that whoever wrote that meant exactly what he said. The psalms are a moving and spiritually rewarding testimony of the encounter between human souls and God—superb for use in worship, but not at every point to be, in Lindbeck's words, "mistakenly viewed as doctrinal definitions." Similarly it can be said of the Creeds that they should not be regarded exclusively as doctrinal definitions, for they also have a liturgical function. The two blend.

The Doctrine of the Gospel

If all this leaves you somewhat confused as to whether lines like "He descended into hell" (which appears in the Nicene Creed as well as the Apostles' Creed) are to be used liturgically or as doctrinal statements, I'm not surprised! I surmise that many Lutherans would give an answer different from that of most Roman Catholics. *The Augsburg Confession,* which is the guide for Lutherans, states in Article VII, "And to the true unity of the Church, it is enough to agree concerning the doctrine of the Gospel and the administration of the Sacraments." But nowhere to my knowledge do the Confessions provide a *precise* definitive statement of what teachings this "doctrine of the Gospel" encompasses. (Article IV of *The Augsburg Confession* dealing with justification is usually regarded as such a definition. I've no doubt that the authors regarded the descent into hell as an authentic part of the Christian faith—Article III clearly states it.) But is it an inseparable part of the gospel, the meaning of which is regarded as essential to the unity of the church? I don't read Scripture that way.

Unanswered Questions

Then if one looks beneath the formal statements of the churches, do Lutherans and Roman Catholics accept the Nicene Creed in the same way? Lindbeck makes a proposal in his paper which, while not covering all aspects of the problem, seems to me to make a lot of sense. He suggests that a general agreement should be regarded as existing if there is (1) rejection of what the dogma clearly and unequivocally rejects, and (2) agreement that what the dogma asserts can be interpreted in an acceptable way. Unfortunately Lindbeck could not be present at the meeting, and his suggestion was not discussed; but the thrust of the dialogue on succeeding topics leads me to surmise that we are not far apart on this point. The two final paragraphs of the joint summary statement acknowledge some unfinished work related to the nature and structure of the teaching authority of the church; the role of Scripture in relation to the teaching office of the church; and the development of doctrine. These are treated extensively in subsequent chapters.

I emphasize that the views I have expressed are my own; no doubt some other Lutherans would disagree with them. Those who do not recognize the points I have raised as issues in their own faith or who, while acknowledging them, prefer not to wrestle with them, have my understanding. For me this discussion brought to the surface the need to articulate an option to faith other than a blind, uncritical embrace of a package of inherited words, many of which I am unable to relate to my living faith in Jesus Christ, God's only-begotten Son, my Redeemer.

Any desire to reflect upon and digest the points raised by the dialogue on the Nicene Creed would take weeks, not hours! Let me summarize some of the main issues, not necessarily in the order of importance:

1. Functions of Creeds—definition, self-identification, worship.
2. Relation of dogmas to Scripture—equal or subordinate?
3. Categories in the hierarchy of dogmas—which are binding?
4. Certification of orthodox Christian teachings—reversible or not?

DISCUSSION

Suggestions for a Discussion of the Nicene Creed

- Have the group read together the Nicene Creed. Inform them that both the Lutheran church and the Roman Catholic Church accept the Nicene Creed.
- Inform the group that the Nicene Creed was written to meet questions of its day. Have the group try to think what are some of the great questions of the church today, for example, do people wonder about who Jesus really was—only human or God or both? Do people have difficulty in putting what they learned in childhood together with what they believe as adults? After identifying the questions, ask whether the Creed answers any of the questions. Does it raise any of the questions?
- You could present this case study for discussion:

  Tom is a third-year student at a local college. He had not attended church for six years. Last Sunday he dropped in at worship at the student center. The Nicene Creed was said. The words were so unusual to his ears he could not believe what he was hearing—"eternally begotten of the Father," . . . "is seated at the right hand of the Father." "He will come . . . to judge the . . . dead," and "Baptism for the forgiveness of sins." After worship he returned to his room, picked up his course book on neurophysiology, and wondered whether he could ever feel right in church again.

  How might he find the connection between what he is reading and what he heard in church?

  The purpose of this discussion is to help the group see that the Creeds were addressed to the concerns of their historical period and not our own.

CHAPTER 2

One Baptism for the Remission of Sins

The Nicene Creed says, "We acknowledge one Baptism for the forgiveness of sins." That acknowledgement means what it says. Lutherans and Catholics agree on Baptism. The joint statement of the co-chairpersons reports: "We were reasonably certain that the teachings of our respective traditions regarding baptism are in substantial agreement, and this opinion has been confirmed at this meeting" (page 85).

But don't be misled by these statements; it wasn't that simple! The issues raised in connection with the subject of Baptism were knotty and were by no means completely resolved. The group did not issue a summary statement, but rather requested two of its members to write accounts of the trends of the discussion and the problems encountered in it. Thus it may be helpful to begin this study with the papers of Warren Quanbeck and Joseph Baker. These in turn will require cross-reference to the biblical, historical, and doctrinal essays of the other writers.

A Summary of Agreements

Quanbeck notes that the two biblical papers agree that "it is essential to see baptism as a rite of initiation, a means of entry into the church, a passage from the old aeon into the new, and that the other biblical statements concerning baptism are to be seen in the light of this fact. Baptism thus has an eschatological [i.e., relating to last things such as resurrection, judgment, everlasting life] and ecclesiological (churchly) significance, relating to God's redeeming deeds for his people. It is also presented as union with Christ in his death and resurrection, and is connected with the gift of the Holy Spirit and with the forgiveness of sins."

. . . and Some Problems

That's quite a package of ideas to be compressed into the term *Baptism!* But anyone familiar with the New Testament writings should be able to identify each of these aspects and relate them in general to the Sacrament of Holy Baptism. The problems arise when one begins to ask questions. Quanbeck lists a few: ". . . the problems of infant baptism and emergency baptism, the relation of baptism to original sin, the necessity of baptism, the minister of baptism, the problem of dominical institution (whether or not commanded by Christ himself), the relation of baptism to penance, to the gifts of the Spirit, to forgiveness, to membership in the church, the relation of the church to the kingdom of God, and the authority of the church to make changes in the mode of baptism" (page 72, parentheses added). And, one might add, why call it a *sacrament?* What's so special about that term?

Authentic Teaching Versus Local Ideas

We'll take up that last question in the next chapter; at the moment we have our hands full enough! Reflecting upon the rites of the church and the variety of ways in which they are understood, I recall two incidents in my parish ministry. One occurred at a cemetery where during the interment proceedings I was deeply moved by the obvious grief of the widow who wept copiously, stretching supplicating arms to heaven in her bereavement. But as we left the cemetery in the undertaker's limousine, she turned to me with a radiant smile and said, "Well, pastor, we put him away right, didn't we?" The other took place during a visit in a home where another baby had just arrived. After I had dutifully admired the newcomer, the mother asked me, "Pastor, how soon should we bring her to the church and have her done?" These were examples of "the-Bible-says-it, so-let's-get-on-with-it" attitude. I hope they were not common examples of parish piety, because in today's times, habit and custom are not enough. We need to have meaning behind what we do. We must make a responsible

Christian witness. We must "always be prepared to make a defense to any one who calls you to account for the hope that is in you" (1 Peter 3:15). We've got to face up to the questions that Baptism may raise even though again we may scare out more rabbits than we can handle.

Development of Doctrine About Baptism

The final point in the summary statement on the Nicene Creed reads, "We together acknowledge that the problem of the development of doctrine is crucial today and is in the forefront of our common concern." A consideration of the meaning and effects of Baptism plunges us into that very concern. How do we say what Baptism is? Although theologians have long been aware of the necessity of grappling with this issue, Lutherans have shied away from it. They tend to be wary of spelling out doctrines or teachings which are not explicitly found in the Bible. They have that hesitation because for generations they have been admonished by the slogan "The Word Alone." Reference was made in the previous chapter to Roman Catholic teaching about the sources of revelation: Sacred Scripture and the divine tradition. This is the place to look at this subject, for this and all subsequent topics involve it in one way or another.

"Professors Brown and Stendahl, who were asked to prepare the biblical papers, came to substantial agreement on what the New Testament says about baptism," reports Quanbeck. The critical questions deal not so much with what the Bible *says* as with what these sayings *imply.* As Quanbeck notes, ". . . there are many difficulties in interpreting the NT references to baptism, inasmuch as they occur not in the context of systematic expositions of the meaning of baptism, but incidentally in relation to the discussion of other problems of the early church" (page 72). By the time the New Testament books were written and assembled, the practice of Baptism was firmly established with many facets of meaning, and the meanings apparently were taken for granted without any group sensing a need to spell them out in a formal way.

Raymond Brown's study is most provocative on this point. He notes that the first three Gospels do not indicate that Jesus baptized anyone; that the reference in John 3:22 which indicated that he did so is "qualified by John 4:2 which states that 'Jesus himself did not baptize, but only his disciples.' "

Brown calls attention to the relation between baptizing with water and with the Spirit and to the fact that the Acts of the Apostles reports instances of the reception of the Spirit, without any Baptism with water. Was Baptism regarded as necessary for salvation? Apparently so, at least for adults, though Brown points out that there is no biblical evidence that all of the apostles were baptized (page 13).

The Factor of Biblical Research

One way out of such difficulties is to try to read between the lines of Scripture—as indeed much biblical scholarship does. But here one can only speak of possibilities or probabilities.

Brown, in speaking of John 3:5, introduces a still more controversial issue. In this chapter, Jesus points out the difference between being begotten of flesh and of Spirit, stating that one must be "born anew" (or as Brown prefers to translate "begotten anew") to see the kingdom of God. In response to Nicodemus' question, Jesus is also quoted as saying that one must be born of water and the Spirit. Brown comments that "The exegete would find it difficult to decide whether this saying comes from Jesus and to what extent it has undergone the refraction of Johannine theology" (page 12). This remark refers to the changes which have apparently been made in the biblical text. The changes are called refractions and have been discovered by biblical scholars. I should add that this type of scholarship is rejected by most fundamentalists who believe that every word of Scripture was literally inspired, if not dictated, by the Holy Spirit. Recent biblical scholarship cannot be given full treatment in these paragraphs; but because of its relation to the development of doctrine, it has to be mentioned.

The Process of Preserving Oral Witness

The issue of the Bible's sources can be simply stated. In the years immediately following Jesus' resurrection, his words and the events of his ministry were passed along by word of mouth. Gradually they were committed to writing. Traces of some of the earlier records which were not preserved can be detected in the first three Gospels. Thus the New Testament as we have it today contains the earliest surviving accounts written by those who remembered Jesus. The accounts were preserved in ancient Greek-language manuscripts. These vary from one to the other, but none of the variations undermines our understanding of the essentials of the Christian faith. But there *are* some variations and insertions, and we do not know when they they were made or by whom. A good example is that of the closing verses of the Gospel According to St. Mark. The Revised Standard Version places them in a footnote, indicating that some early texts include these verses; others do not. This affects our study of Baptism because that text mentions Baptism. In fact it says, "He who believes and is baptized will be saved." The questionable origin of this text is recognized by theologians as conservative as Arthur Carl Piepkorn who observes in his paper for the dialogues that in answering the question "What does Baptism give or profit?" Luther's *Small Catechism* "appeals to the textually dubious passage of Mark 16:16" (page 36). Two paragraphs later, Piepkorn mentions that there are those who entertain at least the possibility "that the Trinitarian formula of St. Matthew 28:19 does not exactly reproduce the expressed command of our Lord, but that it is either the baptismal formula of the particular community within which the First Gospel emerged or a theological specification and interpretation of the baptismal act . . . ." Thus the words "In the name of the Father and of the Son and of the Holy Spirit" which we use in Baptism may themselves have been a later addition to the biblical text.

In Catholic thought, an addition to the Scripture could be an inspired addition, being equal in revelation to the original.

Scripture as a Record of Early Christian Faith

Without going into the claims or counterclaims arising from critical biblical scholarship, we should note two points which are especially important. The first is almost buried in the footnote to Brown's comment on John 3:5: "Besides the problem of whether or not 'water' is an editorial addition (which in Catholic thought would be an inspired editorial addition) . . ." (page 12; see also footnote on page 16). His point appears to be that whenever and by whomever they were written, the books of the New Testament are a reliable, authentic record of the *actual faith* of the Christian communities out of which they came. The apostolic memories of Jesus, which previously had been handed down orally, were thus gradually preserved in writing. By the middle of the second century, there were many such accounts, some of them introducing events or sayings not found in the earlier tradition. Thus the church found it necessary to draw up a list (or canon) of those writings which were regarded as authentic, preserved in their accuracy by the inspiration of the Holy Spirit. This list is gathered in the New Testament as we have it today.

Certification by the Spirit-led Church

All this is fairly elementary. But Brown seems to be touching upon a basic Roman Catholic conviction which some Protestants and some Catholics tend to ignore, namely, that the New Testament was not wrapped, sealed, and delivered by God in one package at one moment in history as is claimed for the Book of Mormon, for example. The Bible was the result of a long development with its final contents—editorial insertions, additions, and all—*certified by the church* as guided by the Holy Spirit. This authority of the church to make such decisions in the belief that it is led by the Holy Spirit will come up time and again in our study. Those who single out the Bible as their sole doctrinal authority *implicitly acknowledge the authority of the Spirit-led church* which decided which books should be included in the New Testament.

There is an instance of the authority of the church in practice. Does the church continue to have the authority? There is no reason to suppose that such authority was cancelled as soon as the canon was established. If the church has that authority, what are its limits? The roots of much misunderstanding and disagreement lie exactly there.

Brown sums it up clearly: ". . . the task of this paper is to *distinguish* between the NT thought and the developments that are a part of the living tradition of his (the New Testament interpreter's) church. As a Catholic he believes that often where the NT is silent on a particular point about baptism, the living tradition of the church may fill in the lacuna [gap] in helping to determine the fullness of apostolic thought, but it is still his duty to point out that the NT *is* silent on this particular point. As a Catholic he believes that the NT cannot teach a doctrine that contradicts the dogmatic formulations of the later church; for since the same Spirit is at work in the NT and the church, the NT and the church in treating of revelation cannot give contradictory answers to the same problem formulated in the same way" (page 10).

The New Testament cannot contradict the church, this says. Protestants would be quick to retort that neither can the church teach a doctrine that is "in formal and direct contradiction with" the New Testament, and Brown would agree. In fact, he states in the succeeding paragraph: ". . . the doctrines or practices of the later church bring out the potentialities of NT thought, and thus cannot be judged to be contradictory to apostolic practice and thought" (page 10).

Tradition and Traditions

What then is the fuss all about? It focuses upon the words, "the living tradition of the church." Which church? Which tradition? There is not much dispute about the teachings of the ecumenical councils prior to the time of the split between the Western and the Eastern churches; for although not all parts of the church were represented at them, all parts subsequently subscribed to them. Since then, what "seemed good to the Holy Spirit and to us" (Acts 15:28) often differed, strikingly so, at the time of the Reformation. The fragmentation of the church garbled its voice in embarrassing ways—it still does.

Infant Baptism as a Tradition

Yet the development of doctrine was a fact of life in the early church, and continues today. This is the second point which needs to be stressed, and infant Baptism is an excellent example of it. Lutherans would do well to take a hard look at it, for in a sense they too have a living tradition; otherwise, what are Lutherans?

The centuries-old dispute about infant Baptism is well described in the papers prepared for the dialogue group. Piepkorn states: "The Lutheran apologetic for infant baptism has always conceded the absense of a direct Dominical [coming from Jesus] (or even apostolic) command to baptize infants in the sacred scriptures" (page 52, brackets added). Biblical scholars are divided on the question as to whether or not infants were baptized in the early decades or even the first century of the church's life. Krister Stendahl agrees with those who rule it out. Brown surmises that references to the Baptism of a household make it plausible that it happened at times, though he is "less sure" that newborn infants were baptized in New Testament times. Apart from a lack of historical evidence, the chief theological obstacle to infant Baptism is the passage from St. Mark, "He who believes and is baptized will be saved." Obviously a baby is incapable of such belief and thus is said by some not to qualify for the benefits of Baptism. As was noted before, Stendahl also comments that this text "belongs to the longer ending of Mark, and is commonly considered secondary by contemporary biblical scholars. The evidence from Acts 2, 8, and 10 clearly indicates that the points about the relation between faith and baptism were not a conscious theological problem in New Testament times."

Limits in the Church's Authority to Develop Doctrine

To regroup for a moment, we started talking about Baptism. We agreed on Baptism, but that agreement gave us the freedom to discuss how we come to know what Baptism really is in the first place. Where do we get our information? How does the information get its authority? Has the church had that authority, or does it come entirely in the Scriptures? We pointed out that the Scriptures are not always clear on the matter of Baptism. That intensifies the question of authority. Where the Scriptures do have rather definite statements, our scholarship has found reason to believe that some of the statements are not necessarily the original text. Some of the statements may have been added. Where is the authority there? In fact, we realized the work of selecting the books that make up the Scriptures was itself done by the authority of the church. That would leave us leaning toward the authority of the church. The Lutherans resist that, however. They believe that the Reformation itself was an attempt to call into question church authority as it had developed and to return to scriptural authority. That is where we are now in this chapter—trying to determine what, if any, authority the Lutherans ascribe to the church. They in turn keep reaching back to the Scripture as a corrective and ultimate authority.

One way of asking the question is, How did doctrine develop? Doctrine developed as a result of reflection upon the teachings of Jesus and their meaning for the church. This process of reflection can be seen already in the Acts of the Apostles and in most of the Epistles. The Lutheran members of the dialogue group were pressed by the Roman Catholic participants regarding the Lutheran understanding of this process as it has continued in the life of the church. They asked what power the church has to decide how Baptism is to be administered. The actual question was (recorded in Quanbeck's paper): "What are the empowerments (i.e., authority to determine or formulate) of the church in regard to the modalities (i.e., ways of defining and administering) of baptism, and what is the relation of confessional statements to the church and scripture? Can they add anything to what scripture says?"

George Lindbeck responded with a series of four theses generally supported by the Lutheran group (also quoted by Quanbeck on pages 75–76, parentheses added). The first two were as follows.

1. The church is empowered to develop new ways of organizing itself, administering the means of grace and formulating authoritative doctrine in view of (a) the needs of the situation in which it finds itself and (b) faithfulness to the scriptural witness. Thus, for example, infant baptism and affusion (i.e., baptism by pouring or sprinkling water rather than by bodily immersion) are legitimate.
2. Developments cannot be dogmatically binding, that is, used as tests of orthodoxy, unless explicitly required by the scriptural witness either (a) in itself, or (b) in confrontation with new post-biblical questions. Nicaea and Chalcedon are dogmatically binding in view of (b) but not (a). Application: (1) The practice of infant baptism cannot be made a dogmatic requirement. (2) Anabaptist dogmatic denial of the validity of infant baptism is also an illegitimate development.

Again we see the Lutheran answer admitting that the church has some authority, but feeling uneasy about it and reaching back to Scripture for the real authority.

Infant Baptism and John 3:5

Lindbeck's second thesis referred to Nicaea and Chalcedon, citing the Nicene Creed itself as an example of development of doctrine. The Lutheran Confessions also could be described, in a sense, as developments in doctrine.

We are discussing how doctrine develops, and we are using infant Baptism as a case in point. The drift of the papers was that teachings regarding infant Baptism must be in harmony with Scripture, but, further, are based upon ecclesiastical, theological, and pastoral considerations. Piepkorn's paper spells out these considerations in detail from the Lutheran point of view. Stendahl asserts that "baptism in the New Testament and in the early church is always an act of *initiation*" (a fact also mentioned by Brown). We can see the initiation coming up in John 3:5, "Unless one is begotten of water and the spirit, he cannot enter the kindgom of God." For those taking that literally, the denial of Baptism to infants would jeopardize their salvation. How else could one interpret it literally? On the other hand, in dealing with this passage, Brown says, "There is no evidence that the author was concerned with denying the kingdom of God to those who through no fault of their own are unbaptized. His immediate concern was one of contrasting flesh and Spirit, and of insisting that life from above is not the same as ordinary life and cannot be received without the work of the Spirit. His 'unless' refers to the general incapacity of the purely natural. Therefore we should be careful to avoid interpreting New Testament thought on the necessity of Baptism in the light of the later (Augustinian) problematic, for the New Testament does not speculate on the fate of the unbaptized. What the New Testament does stress is that in order for an adult to pass from the kingdom of death, darkness, falsehood, and Satan into the kingdom of life, light, truth—in short into the kingdom of God—he must be baptized."

The Doctrinal Development

Just as Brown writes that "the church came to believe that baptism in water *and* Spirit was the fulfillment of the promise that Jesus would baptize with a Holy Spirit" (page 13), so the church *came to believe* that infants should be baptized. As Piepkorn puts it: "Because baptism is a divine gift of which man stands in dire need, it is not something which the church has in her competence to administer or withhold, but which she must administer and to which the Christian has a right for himself and for his children" (page 53).

The Factor of Faith

But the question of the relation of Baptism to faith remains. Some years ago when remaining in Minneapolis over a week-end for some meetings, I attended an early Roman Catholic mass and thereafter went to a Baptist service. Quite a contrast! It happened that on that day, Baptist parents brought infants to the front of the church for what as I recall was described as "dedication" or "consecration." I clearly remember the remarks of the pastor in connection with this procedure. He laid great stress on the point that *nothing actually happened to the infant* in what took place. The important thing was that the church prayed that God would so guide and bless the child in its years ahead that he or she would develop the faith which would eventually make the benefits of Baptism possible, and that the parents would commit themselves to help the child acquire that faith.

Contrast that with the Lutheran view that God is willing to come to the child completely free before the child can show any faith. In the words of Piepkorn: "As the child is carried to the font, it is incapable of meeting any precondition. It does not have contrition; it does not have faith; it does not have the intention of receiving a sacrament; it cannot comprehend or respond to a proclamation of the Gospel. What is more, the minister of the sacrament may be immoral and unrepentant. The sponsors that represent the church may be members of the holy community *nomine tantum non re* (in name, but not in fact). Whatever happens in baptism must be God's work. Thus infant baptism becomes a paradigm of God's dealing with man" (page 51). "In infant baptism we see . . . divine grace operating most explicitly and most dramatically. Here God, on the basis of his predestination and vocation, makes a child of wrath, who has been able to do nothing toward his own salvation, his own child and imparts to him by sheer grace the sonship that the eternally begotten Son possesses by nature" (pages 51–52). In short, something happens by the action of God's grace.

Searching Out the Meaning of Scripture

An analysis of God's grace in infant Baptism is not found explicitly in any one section of the Scripture, but is gleaned in the total perspective of the gospel. This is an example of development of doctrine, and as such, is subject to divided opinion.

Luther is not always at his best in dealing with this issue. He begins the section entitled "Infant Baptism" in the *Large*

Catechism by saying, "Let the simple dismiss this question from their minds, and refer it to the learned." He then goes on to argue that God has sanctified many who have been thus baptized and given them the Holy Spirit; otherwise the church would not have survived. His main insistence is that faith does not make Baptism, but receives it; "everything depends upon the Word and commandment of God." Just how the faith of an infant receives it, he does not say. Later on he begins a sentence, "For (as we have said) even though infants did not believe, which, however, is not the case (as we shall now prove) . . . ," but one looks in vain for the promised proof. In fact, he writes, "We bring the child in the purpose and hope that it may believe, and we pray that God may grant it faith: but we do not baptize it upon that, but solely upon the command of God." Bringing the child in hope that it will believe, and praying that God may grant it faith? That is exactly what I saw the Baptists do. But Luther does not baptize the child on those conditions. That is where Luther and the Baptists interpret the Scriptures differently. Lutherans and Roman Catholics agree on infant Baptism.

Piepkorn interprets Luther's position in this way: " 'To have faith' in the context of infant baptism thus means to have become a person in whom God has initiated his work of sanctification and to whom he has given the Holy Spirit. As the individual matures, the Holy Spirit enables him so to see in the divine word God's revelation of his gracious self and of his saving purpose in Christ that the individual comes to know, trust in, and worship Christ . . ." (page 47). Later on in youth, both Lutherans and Roman Catholics administer confirmation, (a *rite* for the former and a *sacrament* for the latter), as a sign of growth in the Spirit and nurture by the church, the Body where faith is located. God's promise and grace bestowed in Baptism is witnessed publicly in personal testimony and commitment.

Varieties in Interpretations

One who reads Piepkorn's analysis from the Lutheran Confessions may get lost in the language of the sixteenth century. Quanbeck's report on the dialogues contains a key paragraph on this aspect, which is worth pondering: "It was noted that the Council of Trent and the *Formula of Concord* say substantially the same things about baptism, and that contemporary theology in both traditions affirms what has been asserted in the past and at the same time seeks other language for the exposition of the doctrine of baptism today. This is so because of the more adequate biblical scholarship in our day and because the questions raised in modern experience of the world are asked out of different presuppositions and from different perspectives. Thus a Lutheran finds himself in continuity with the presentation of the doctrine of sin in the Lutheran Confessions and at the same time finds the categories of the sixteenth-century theology too individualistic and too impersonal to do justice to the teachings of the Scriptures. He stands with the Reformers as they face the questions asked by their century, and he also seeks new formulations to meet the questions raised today." The Lutheran Church in America's major doctrinal statement on Baptism presented in the Report on The Study of Theological Affirmations at the 1974 Convention does just this. It used today's language to discuss today's questions in the light of the church's historical understandings of Baptism.

A specific example of the language problem arises when considering the remission of sins as an effect of Baptism. Regarding this, Quanbeck raises the same question: "Here again it became clear that Roman Catholics and Lutherans say many of the same things about sin and forgiveness, and are also alike in their uneasiness about certain tradition formulations. The historical study of the Scriptures, for example, raises questions about the traditional statement of the doctrine of original sin. At least in its popular expositions it is too individualistic and inadequately personal to do justice to the scriptural teachings. Similarly the new appreciation of the eschatological language of the Scriptures has called into question many of the temporal or dogmatic sequences posited by theologians in the life of the believer" (page 74).

More baffling language for the nontheologian! Enough to say that Roman Catholics and Lutherans say the same things about sin and forgiveness. Enough to say that they are also alike in their uneasiness about language of past centuries. Quanbeck does not pursue the matter farther, and I certainly should not put words in his mouth.

But it is not enough to bring up original sin and say no more. Piepkorn writes: "Baptism applies to the individual the reconciliation and pardon that God in Christ achieved for the whole world of mankind. This forgiveness includes the remission of original sin, understood as the removal of the guilt, but not of the 'matter' of original sin" (page 38). But Brown states: "Indeed, the whole problem of original sin in the Augustinian sense does not seem to enter into NT baptismal thought" (page 15). A look at the doctrine of original sin quickly plunges us into the way in which the Bible is understood and interpreted, a subject which cannot be treated fully here, but which nevertheless cannot be left out completely.

The doctrine of original sin plunges us into many thoughts. Article II of *The Augsburg Confession* states: "It is also taught among us that since the fall of Adam all men who are born according to the course of nature are conceived and born in sin. That is, all men are . . . unable by nature to have true fear of God and true faith in God. Moreover, this inborn sickness and hereditary sin is truly sin and condemns to the eternal wrath of God all those who are not born again through Baptism and the Holy Spirit." So also with St. Paul. He writes in Romans 5:17: "If, because of one man's trespass, death reigned through that one man, much more will those who receive the abundance of grace and the free gift of righteousness reign in life through the one man Jesus Christ."

When the subject of original sin comes up, many rabbits appear from the bushes, and they are rabbits we have to deal with immediately or we'll get nothing else done.

Some of My Own Reflections on Original Sin

Let's go back to the Fall in the sequences of this drama. The first humans, getting off to a clean start, disobey God and fall into sin, a condition passed on to all succeeding generations. The wage of this sin is death. (This *original sin* is the "disease or vice of origin" spoken of in *The Augsburg Confession,* which automatically condemns every human being. Baptism then comes along to remove the guilt of this sin, but not the inclination of this sin. We still want to continue sinning.)

Christ, the second Adam, also had a clean start. Conceived by the Holy Spirit, born of a virgin, he did not have the guilt and subsequent condition of original sin. He too was tempted by Satan, but remained sinless and triumphed where the first Adam had failed. He nevertheless suffered death, but because he was the blameless God-human, his self-offering was and is accepted as expiation for the sins of each person who in repentance and faith accepts him as Savior. Thus the very *Law,* which condemns us is fulfilled and gives way to the *Grace* of the gospel, the good news of the victory of the second Adam.

This summary of the divine drama is all too brief and oversimplified to do it justice, but it recites the sequence we have heard again and again. The summary is true to the historical teachings, and yet there is something in it which doesn't come off in our day. Not that it is untrue; indeed it is a profound truth. But its language would baffle a student in freshman biology, if not in law. We don't sacrifice many animals for the retribution of the law, though we do sacrifice them vicariously for medical research. The old language even gives theologians some halt. It may be "too individualistic and inadequately personal to do justice to the scriptural teaching" (page 74 Quanbeck).

To be sure, the basis for these sequences can be found in the Scriptures, but there are other biblical insights about reconciliation and salvation which don't fit into this neat, almost legalistic transaction with its Old Testament sacrificial overtones. To assert that early Christians received the truths of the gospel in terms of the thought-forms and historical understandings of their era is not to deny these truths, but only to distinguish between the insights as such and the cultural conditioning of the language and symbols through which they are expressed. Truth revealed in the Scriptures can be conveyed through more than one mode of expression.

Old Truths Seen in New Perspectives

Why have we gotten onto the subject of updating language? Because we are about to pose the thought that the Holy Spirit continuously clarifies the truth about Jesus Christ in today's language without changing the central meaning of that truth. Could that be why different words are used from age-to-age by the same Holy Spirit without contradiction of the same Holy Spirit?

Quanbeck noted (as quoted above) that "the questions raised in modern experience of the world are asked out of different presuppositions and from different perspectives" (page 73) than those of the past. With respect to the doctrine of original sin, can we properly seek new formulations to meet the questions raised today? Or, as we have just now put it, can we believe that the Holy Spirit guides and safeguards the church today in a development of doctrine which clarifies the truth of the gospel in Jesus Christ as given us in the Scriptures, without changing the central meaning of that truth?

The traditional teaching about original sin, which certainly aided the early church to understand what God had done for humanity through Jesus Christ, made its point adequately. What happens, however, when many contemporary Christians (including myself) do not regard the Garden of Eden as a geographical place, nor the fall of Adam and Eve as an historical event, but rather accept this section of Genesis as profound revealed insights regarding the nature of the entire human family and of its relationship to the Creator God? Disregarding the geography of Eden does not mean disbelieving the concept of a universal, insidious, and pervasive sin which burdens every member of the human race, and which condemns to death. I firmly share this understanding of the human condition. I *know* that I have been self-centered and selfish from the earliest moments of my self-awareness, and I have observed it in the youngest children even before self-awareness is evident. If you have ever wanted desperately to do something that you knew was wrong, you know what I'm talking about. I'm not talking about simple physical desire. I'm talking about the desire to get what I want no matter how much it costs others, that is, the desire to be first on my list. It's a desire that goes to the very core of one's being. That self-centeredness is the original vice. This is indeed a curse and requires salvation from its consequences.

But the idea that I must accept a responsibility for this "vice of origin," resulting in "guilt," which can be removed by Baptism, does not seem to me to "do justice to the scriptural teachings," as a whole. As Brown puts it: ". . . NT thought is not rigorously consistent on the action that brings about the remission or cleansing of sin and Christian renewal" (page 21).

It all means that we can sense the central truth while we are given some room to move around in the words, and this doesn't contradict the Holy Spirit; it is the Holy Spirit at work.

The Corporate Context

In my own search for a fuller understanding of the biblical teachings about Baptism, I find help in one of Quanbeck's comments quoted above, namely, that the traditional teaching about original sin, at least in its popular expositions, "is too individualistic and inadequately personal." Something happens to an individual in Baptism, but it occurs as a part of a group. It occurs in a corporate context, an aspect which must never be detached if it is to be fully understood. A child is never just born. Rather, endowed with an incredibly complex human heritage of physical, mental, and emotional characteristics, he or she enters a maze of human relationships. She or he is born *into the human family,* with all the meaning that term conveys and without which the birth would be meaningless. So, likewise, a child is never just baptized (or in the words of my parishioner, "done"), but rather is baptized *into the church.* Far from being an isolated individual with the millstone of original sin hanging around his or her neck, a child sharing the selfish, self-centered drives of the entire human family is incorporated into the Body of Christ where God's grace and the power of the gospel are ever at work. Baptism isn't just a momentary encounter between grace and faith, but the beginning of a life-long process of living with relationships within the corporate context of the Christian family. This is why the theologians call it an *initiation.*

In Piepkorn's words (page 44): "By being incorporated into the holy community the person baptized [infant or adult] participates in the circulation of Christ's own life that flows through all of the body of Christ" (brackets added). Speaking of infant Baptism, the *New Catechism* published by Roman Catholics in Holland declares: "But the question is how can the child receive the sign of conversion and faith while it is still incapable of conversion and of the dedication of faith, for lack of mental equipment. The answer is that it receives the sign in the way in which it lives—in dependence on adults. Christ made his salvation a community matter, a social thing. He did not give it to individuals in isolation from each other, but to a people . . . . We bring the children within the circle of our own faith, into the faith of the church."

This dimension of the meaning of Baptism is grounded in the Scriptures too, and adds to the inexhaustible richness of the ways in which God reaches out to his people.

No one in his or her right mind should claim to have the final answers to all these questions wrapped up in a neat set of formulas. The dialogue group did not attempt to formulate a full explication of Baptism, but wanted to be sure that Lutherans and Roman Catholics are not divided on the subject. I have given greater attention to *infant* Baptism since it is more difficult and leads inescapably into the major issue of the development of doctrine. One must never forget that personal presuppositions, whatever their source, cannot limit the ways in which God speaks to and acts upon his people through the gospel and his Spirit-led Body, the church.

So you see, while the subject of Baptism seemed easy, the issues related to it are far from simple.

Dilemmas for discussion:

1. The authority of the Scriptures. Do some Scripture texts have more authority than others?
2. The authority of the church to choose which books would make up the New Testament canon. Is that the same authority as the one used to develop subsequent doctrine in harmony with the Scriptures?
3. The language used to establish doctrine. Does the Holy Spirit use different words at different eras of history?
4. The group meaning of Baptism. How can individual piety take on a more corporate growth?

DISCUSSION

Suggestions for a Discussion of Baptism

- You could have the group discuss this case study:

  Jan was baptized in the hospital because she was not expected to live. Her parents were not active church members. Jan grew up with some idea of what the Christian faith was about. As she became older she occasionally read the Bible, and she went to worship fairly regularly. But basically she thought that faith was mostly what she herself personally believed because her parents had always said it is what you believe in your heart that counts.
  Christy was baptized at a worship service with 160 persons present. She grew up spending many hours a week in one kind of church gathering or another. When she was older she seldom thought about what she actually believed; but she did go to worship fairly regularly. She felt a sense of confidence in being a part of the church as she joined the worshipers in saying the Creed, prayed for forgiveness, and heard the reading of the Scripture.

  Which do you think represents the Christian faith better, a care about individual beliefs or a care about being a part of the church community? Which do participants identify with more?

- Have the group read Mark 16:15, 16. Read it from the Revised Standard Version Common Bible, if a copy is available. You might mention that this is a translation considered acceptable by both Catholics and Protestants. After reading the verses, have the group notice the footnote, if there is one in their Bible. The footnote points out that some of the oldest copies of the Gospel of Mark include these verses and some do not.

  Ask members of the group whether they consider these verses to be any less authoritative since they were not part of the original text. How can they decide what is to be accepted as absolutely true and what is open to question?

- Have the group look at the apocryphal books of the Bible, that is, those located between Malachi and Matthew. Some churches give more authority to these books than do other churches. Which is of greater authority: the books of the Bible or the churches that choose which books should be in the Bible?

- Have the group discuss whether they believe infants should be baptized and why or why not? List the reasons on the chalkboard. After the list is on the chalkboard, beside each reason write what authority was used to arrive at the reason—implications in Scripture, the church's practice, the reasoning of the mind, feelings?

  The purpose in all this is to help group members become increasingly aware of what they subscribe to as their authority. They may note a difference between personal ascription to authority and ecclesiastical ascription to authority. The church as a group must have a common authority; individuals, however, may have a certain degree of freedom. This distinction will become more and more important in later sessions.

CHAPTER 3

The Eucharist as Sacrifice

The term *Eucharist* is not familiar to many Lutherans, although it appears in the Lutheran Confessions. The word eucharist is derived from the Greek word meaning thanksgiving. For Roman Catholics it may be used in a broad sense to include the entire worship service commonly called the Mass. In a more technical sense it is used to mean a portion of the Mass. The Mass consists of the *Service of the Word* and the *Service of the Table.* The latter is styled the Eucharist proper. The Lutheran equivalent of the latter is the Lord's Supper or Holy Communion, which is not always celebrated at every Sunday or major worship service. In this chapter, the term *Eucharist* is restricted to the Service of the Table, and thus is synonymous with the Lord's Supper.

As the dialogue moved along, the group became ready to grapple with a more controversial subject. The subject chosen was the Eucharist as a sacrifice. This had to do with the presence of Christ who had died on the cross as a sacrifice for our sins. The issue has a double focus: The Lutherans were suspicious of the Catholic emphasis on sacrifice, and feared that the Mass had come to be regarded as a new "unbloody" sacrifice each time it was performed, which augmented or replaced by human efforts the once-for-all sacrifice of Jesus on the cross. The Catholics, on the other hand, were dubious whether Lutherans really believed that Jesus Christ who died for us at Calvary was in any way present in the celebration of the Lord's Supper—in spite of Lutheran emphasis on the "real presence."

What, if Anything, Has Changed?

The sixteenth-century debate on this subject was fierce. Luther wrote, "As the greatest of all abominations, I regard the mass when it is preached or sold as a sacrifice or good work." Roman Catholics today point out that what Luther opposed was not and is not the official teaching of their church. They concede that there were abuses and distortions which he rightfully condemned, but they hold that the theological concept of Christ's presence and sacrificial role at each eucharistic celebration is a valid doctrine drawn from Scripture. Furthermore, with reference to "presence" they ask, quite properly, what in fact Lutherans believe happens when they celebrate the Lord's Supper. If they insist upon the real *presence* of him who said: " 'This is my body, which is for you,' " (1 Corinthians 11:23), what do they believe happens?

In its joint statement, the dialogue group declares: "We are no longer able to regard ourselves as divided in the one holy catholic and apostolic faith on these two points" (sacrifice and presence). Does this mean Luther was wrong? Has the Roman Catholic position changed? Do major differences remain which have been glossed over? Or could it be that the two traditions have more in common on this subject than has been recognized?

Discussions on this subject required three meetings over a span of nearly two years. More background studies were needed than for both of the preceding topics combined. At points they are quite technical and, unfortunately for most lay persons (and not a few pastors!), are laced with citations in Greek, Latin, German, and even Hebrew. Yet they bristle with stimulating and creative ideas.

Reason in the Realm of Faith

A Catholic participant described the Eucharist as dealing with the heart of Christianity. It is a mystery—a word which should turn nobody off, for life itself falls into that category; and the meaning both of life and of the Eucharist is unfolded in the realm of faith. This, however, by no means excuses a rational person from trying to clarify the concepts and actions by which that faith is expressed. Such a process brings risks, for what has been taken for granted may—upon careful scrutiny—become more fuzzy than clear. I myself, like most others, still have questions which cry out for answers.

Limits and Procedures

The dialogue group did not make a comprehensive study of the Eucharist, but confined attention to the role of Christ therein with respect to his *sacrifice* and *presence*. The two are intimately related. The sacrifice concept was the major issue in the sixteenth century; but, curiously enough, the presence concept has turned out in succeeding periods to be the more difficult to resolve.

In the printed volume on this topic, the study papers and summary statement are preceded by lucid accounts of the discussions from the viewpoints of Kent Knutson (who subsequently became president of the American Lutheran Church and suffered a tragic death after a brief time in office) and Harry McSorley. These accounts provide helpful perspectives. Especially to be noted at this point is McSorley's comment about how dialogues between churches work. "On so many issues Christians have emotionally reacted against slogans or characteristic phraseology of other Christians without giving evidence that they understood the meaning attached to this language by those who used it. 'Faith and grace alone,' 'scripture alone,' 'the Eucharist is a propitiatory sacrifice' are examples of such traditionally divisive slogans. When one asks, "What do you *mean* when you say that we are justified by faith alone or that the Mass is a propitiatory sacrifice?" one often finds a much greater possibility of agreement than existed when one operated on the pre-ecumenical level of simply opposing one emotion-laden slogan to another" (page 18).

Sacrifice in the Eucharist—Action of God or Church?

Relating Christ's sacrifice to the Lord's Supper is not strange to Lutherans—quite the contrary! The liturgy and hymns we use in celebrating the sacrament refer to this concept repeatedly. How else could one understand the repetition of the words, "O Christ, Thou Lamb of God that takest away the sin of the world, have mercy upon us," and similarly the meaning of the lines sung so frequently:

Draw near and take the body of the Lord
And drink the holy Blood for you outpoured.

Offered was he for greatest and for least,
Himself the victim and himself the priest.

With heav'nly bread makes those who hunger whole,
Gives living waters to the thirsty soul.

The judge eternal, unto whom shall bow
All nations at the last, is with us now.

The problem was not the notion of sacrifice as central to the understanding of the eucharistic action, but rather the question of *who* does *what*. Luther was fiercely opposed to any interpretation which said that forgiveness could be secured by something humans do. He was reacting against the idea that in the Mass, the *church* through the priest offered the crucified body and blood of Christ to God in repetition of Calvary, thereby evoking God's mercy and forgiveness. This was not an official Roman Catholic teaching, but in the sixteenth century most people thought it was.

Had Luther missed the point by attacking a doctrine of the Mass as sacrifice not really held by Roman Catholics? Not necessarily, at least not according to one contemporary Roman Catholic theologian quoted by James McCue: "It is an unwarranted reflection on some of the keenest minds of the age to suppose that the Reformers' whole protest was based on the crass misapprehension that their opponents really claimed to slay Christ daily" (page 47). The writer implies that the opponents really did claim to slay Christ daily.

In more recent times, Protestants have continued to be troubled by claims made by some Roman Catholics. For example, the joint statement refers to a modern, though pre-Vatican II, Catholic theologican who said that "the sacrificial worth of two Masses is just double the sacrificial worth of one Mass." The point of the Reformers was that Christ's sacrifice on Calvary was a once-for-all and sufficient event *accomplished by God* in his will to provide a means for salvation, something which could not be added to or subtracted from, reenacted or offered by any human being or institution. As Luther put it: "We should, therefore, give careful heed to this word 'sacrifice,' so that we do not presume to give God something in the sacrament, when it is he who in it gives us all things" (McCue, page 57).

A Misunderstanding Corrected

On this issue, the air seems to have been cleared. Knutson states: "Lutherans have often understood Roman Catholics to say that the Mass adds to Calvary, is a 're-doing' of Calvary and by this have implied that the one sacrifice of Christ is defective and incomplete. . . . Now we can agree that this is not what Roman Catholics intend to say. The sacrifice of Christ is complete and unalterable and cannot be supplemented or completed by any subsequent action. Rather, that sacrifice, complete in itself, is made *present, made effective* and the *benefits communicated* in the Eucharist'' (page 13, emphases added).

In the preceding paragraph of this same account, Knutson spells out an understanding of sacrifice which he states Lutherans can accept: ''Roman Catholics have called the Mass a sacrifice. They mean by this that the Eucharist is a gracious act in which God makes present and communicates this propitiatory sacrifice for man. This is not a new, or different sacrifice but the same sacrifice of Calvary. The Mass is properly, and necessarily, called sacrifice because the Christ who is the sacrifice is present in the Supper. Sacrificial language, such as 'given for you' and 'shed for you' is used in the Words of Institution, and the whole understanding of the character of God's work for man is brought into focus in this cultic act which communicates God's grace to man. Lutherans agree when the Mass is understood in this way'' (pages 12–13).

Theological Interpretations of the Atonement

This is all to the good. But to clarify *what happens* when the sacrifice of Christ is re-presented or ''made present'' at the celebration of the Lord's Supper, we must examine the several meanings of the term *sacrifice.* St. Paul relates that it was of central importance from the very beginning of Christianity: ''For I delivered to you *as of first importance* what I also received, that Christ died for our sins in accordance with the scriptures . . .'' (1 Corinthians 15:3). How does Christ's death on the cross atone for our sins? This question came only indirectly within the scope of the discussions, but we are forced to discuss it when we talk about a re-presentation of Calvary at Holy Communion. Knutson comments that ''further discussion of the nature of the atonement itself would be helpful.'' Earlier he had stated that the word *sacrifice* is ''not wedded exclusively to an Anselmian understanding of the atonement,'' and that it has ''a much earlier tradition,'' and "is meant to incorporate all the rich implications and interpretations of the atonement found in the Scriptures" (page 12).

The Substitutionary Theory

Both Anselm, a medieval theologian, and John Calvin at the time of the sixteenth-century Reformation, emphasized a substitutionary interpretation of the atonement. A concise summary of their views is given in Quanbeck's previously mentioned *Search for Understanding* (page 95): "Interpreting Christ's work as sacrifice has caused difficulties for theologians for centuries. They seemed to have lost an understanding or feeling for what sacrifice is in the realm of religion, and had sounded like tone deaf men writing music criticism. Anselm offered an interpretation of sacrifice for the men of his time that made use of ideas of the honor of God, and the satisfaction due to his honor, ideas common in feudalism and the code of chivalry. He interpreted the death of Christ as supplying the satisfaction due to God's honor on behalf of men, who because of their sin and guilt were unable to satisfy it. John Calvin later offered another set of pictures, building upon the image of the wrath and judgment of God upon sin. Christ stands in man's place before the righteous judgment of God, and endures the punishment which is due to men. Thus the cost of human sin has been paid, and men can through faith in Christ enter the presence of God not as enemies but as Sons."

The Sacrifice Motif in Scripture

There is considerable scriptural basis for such understandings of the atonement. One can cite many passages, such as Hebrews 9:22—"Indeed, under the law almost everything is purified with blood, and without the shedding of blood there is no forgiveness of sins" or Romans 3:25—". . . Christ Jesus whom God put forward as an expiation by his blood" or Ephesians 1:7—"In him we have redemption through his blood." This motif is found in many other places and is probably the one reflected most in Christian liturgies, hymns, and popular piety. When St. Paul says that Christ died for our sins in accordance with the Scriptures, one must remember that he was speaking of the *Hebrew* Scriptures. The first Christians were Jews, steeped in the history, rites, traditions, and conceptual patterns of their religious heritage. They recognized in

Christ the fulfillment of such passages as Isaiah 53 with its vivid portrayal of the redemptive "suffering servant" on whom "the Lord has laid the iniquity of us all." They saw in Calvary the once-for-all fulfillment of the sacrificial system of Israel.

In their biblical studies, both Jerome Quinn and Bertil Gaertner see close relationships between Jesus' words at the Last Supper and Old Testament rituals. Quinn describes those words as a *declaratory formula.* "With it, he [Jesus] assumes the role of a priest of Israel and proclaims the sacrificial character of his own imminent death" (page 44, brackets added). Gaertner affirms flatly: "There is no doubt that the eucharist in the New Testament is closely related to the death of Christ as a sacrifice. . . . The offering motif is indissolubly connected with the eucharist, since Christ is present in the eucharist not only as the risen and living Son of God but also as the Son put to death for the sins of men" (page 27).

A Contemporary Perspective

Anselm's view was that Christ died as a substitute to satisfy God. How does one respond to those who regard this as an absurd legalistic explanation set in ritualistic imagery? Such persons say that it caricatures God as a proud or angry deity who has to be placated; they say that it uses a human illustration of a human compromise to gain a human solution. Many proponents of this theory are committed Christians who find substitutionary explanations of the atonement inadequate in relation to other biblical insights about God's love, pity, and mercy.

In his book mentioned earlier, Quanbeck suggests: "Sacrifice is not a system of barter in which men offer gifts to God in the hope that his anger will be appeased and he will look upon them with favor. God needs neither men's gifts nor is he susceptible to bribes. He loves his creatures in spite of their disobedience, and moves out in persuasive love to win them back to himself. His justice or wrath stands in the way of man's restoration, not in the sense that God's feelings have been hurt and his injured vanity is in need of appeasement, but because the world has been made with a certain structure. Man has been made for fellowship and harmony with God, and can develop his possibilities as a human being only in this relationship. Sin is man's choice of himself and his own autonomy rather than the context of life in God. And the judgment of sin is not God striking the evil doer in petulant fury, but man's discovery, the hard way, that his life just doesn't function properly when it is lived egocentrically. . . .

"The meaning of sacrifice is thus not to buy God's favor, but to offer one's self to God by identification with the offering which is placed on the altar. . . . Only in Christ is sacrifice offered in reality and in truth. . . . Only by our union with Christ are we able to participate in complete self-offering to God, and thus begin in Christ to become genuine human beings."[1]

A Personal Reaction (Which the Reader May Skip)

For me, this is not an instance in which faith demands an either/or choice—a choice between whether the substitutionary theory is true or false. Surely attempts to discount or discard all aspects of this explanation would take a great treasury from the storehouse of Christian insights. In spite of its negative aspects, it conveys a profound, powerful revelation regarding the awful consequences of sin, the high costs of redemption, and the depth of God's involvement as Redeemer. It has served well to communicate the gospel over a span of many centuries, and continues today to provide spiritual nourishment to persons in all parts of the church. For one who takes the Bible seriously, it cannot be detached from the scriptural witness. Obviously it has to be framed in human concepts—what other kinds are available?

At the same time I am grateful that the Scriptures offer additional insights about atonement. Many scholars point out that Christ's sacrifice did not take place just on Calvary, it included his incarnation and entire life of obedience and love —culminating not in the crucifixion, but in the resurrection. Most helpful to me is the passage in John 3, through verses 16 and 17. In speaking to Nicodemus about entering the kingdom of God, Jesus seems to be concerned less about how God can be enabled to forgive sins than about how a sinner can become a different kind of person. He zeros in on the effects of forgiveness in human beings with words readily understand-

1. Warren A. Quanbeck, *Search for Understanding: Lutheran Conversations with Reformed, Anglican, and Roman Catholic Churches* (Minneapolis: Augsburg Publishing House, 1972), p. 95ff.

able to twentieth-century minds; I can identify myself in them. That which is born only of the flesh remains flesh; its nature is to be self-centered with all the vices which flow out of self-indulgence, greed, and self-worship. By passing the question of exactly how atonement for sins actually committed is accomplished, Jesus gets to the heart of the matter: In order to get at the roots of sin, *human nature* must be transformed; persons must be born of the Spirit.

This does not mean that this gives a person a direct pipeline to the Holy Spirit—a kind of intercom system from heaven which pipes down better advice to change the person. No, the rest of that third chapter of John continuously focuses upon the Lordship of Christ to whom a person's will is submitted. The person is made better by Christ, not by advice. By becoming Lord of my life, Christ does for me what I by myself cannot do. He begins his transforming work in me. His sacrifice of incarnation, obedient servanthood, and vicarious death, followed by his resurrection has rescued me from the death of the flesh. By faith I have been incorporated into fellowship with him, a new relationship initiated at Baptism. Thus it is not God who has to be placated and reconciled to me; it is I who in Christ can be reconciled to God. As St. Paul puts it (Galatians 2:20), "I have been crucified with Christ; it is no longer I who live, but Christ who lives in me; and the life I now live in the flesh I live by faith in the Son of God, who loved me and gave himself for me." This view is also present in the dialogue statement which affirms that Christians are "united through Christ with God and with one another in such a way that they become participants in his worship, his self-offering, his sacrifice to the Father" (page 189).

This scriptural approach to Christ's sacrifice draws my response of faith more readily than does the substitutionary formula, though I do not disregard the latter. The point is that the emphasis on the "making present" of the sacrifice of Christ when the Lord's Supper is celebrated ought to be preceded by awareness of the many dimensions of that sacrifice and of how Christ saves us. The One who comes to me in a special way in the Supper, which undeniably focuses upon Calvary, is not just the sacrificial Lamb of God, but also my Lord whose life, teachings, example, death, and resurrection have captured my heart, and who has incorporated me in his Body, the Church.

The Common Statement on Sacrifice

The common statement issued from the dialogue lists two agreements and four disagreements now diminishing; that is, it lists two affirmations common to both traditions and four aspects of the problem which have been major points of divergence in the past, but which now seem to be in harmony or moving toward convergence.

There is complete agreement that " 'in the Lord's Supper Christ is present as the Crucified who died for our sins and who rose again for our justification, as the once-for-all sacrifice for the sins of the world who gives himself to the faithful.' " Also there is agreement that "the celebration of the eucharist is the church's sacrifice of praise and self-offering or oblation" (page 188).

With respect to the dispute over whether or not the church "offers Christ" in the Mass, both Lutherans and Catholics affirm that the sacrifice of the cross is unrepeatable. "Yet in this memorial we do not only recall past events: God makes them present through the Holy Spirit, thus making us participants in Christ. . . . Through this union between Christ and Christians, the eucharistic assembly 'offers Christ' by consenting in the power of the Holy Spirit to be offered by him to the Father. Apart from Christ we have no gifts, no worship, no sacrifice of our own to offer to God" (pages 189–190).

Remaining differences include the Roman Catholic doctrine that the Mass is also a propitiatory sacrifice for the dead and that it can be a private Mass—said by the priest alone, with whatever that might imply. It is noted, however, that with respect to the prayer for the dead, the *Apology of the Augsburg Confession* states "We do not forbid it," and that with respect to the private Mass, Vatican II declares that the communal way of celebrating the Mass is to be preferred to individual and quasi-private celebrations. These points were not pursued in depth, not being considered central to the issue at hand. In short, the summary statement says that we gather together in the Lord's Supper not only to remember what Christ in his total ministry did for us and for all humanity in the past, but also so that as we receive the Christ who comes to us now in a special way through this sacramental action, the effective benefits of his sacrifice are intensified in us.

Sacramental Action

But what about that adjective *sacramental*? The terms *sacramental action* and *sacramental presence* appear frequently in the documents. As we turn our attention to the subject of "presence" it is necessary to examine the nature and function of sacraments. How may one understand Knutson's declaration that "A sign or symbol is never 'merely' such; but a sacramental sign is always effective, it always communicates what it promises"? (page 15). For example, we might think of a sign like a kiss. It conveys the very touch of affection it symbolizes.

The Lutheran Confessions describe sacraments as ceremonies or acts in which God offers us the content of the promise joined to the ceremony. The three elements are a divine command, the use of an earthly element, and a promise of justifying or saving grace. On the basis of these criteria, Lutherans generally list only two sacraments: Baptism and Holy Communion (although the Lutheran Confessions at times ascribe a sacramental character to penance and, in some respects, to ordination).

The Dutch *New Catechism* speaks of the sacraments as symbols of life, outward signs in which Christ wills to meet us. They are " 'efficacious' signs which do not merely speak of redemption but bring it to us." Using different criteria, Roman Catholics list seven sacraments: Baptism, Eucharist, Confirmation, Marriage, Ordination, Penance, and Extreme Unction (Anointing of the Sick).

The Function of Signs

Both Lutherans and Roman Catholics were once wary about using the terms *sign* or *symbol* when speaking of the sacraments. If signs are construed to signify something remote in time and removed in space, then that something would lack local, current reality. You immediately see the problem this has for the idea of a "real presence." Why symbolize something which is really present? Yet, today these words are recognized as having an essential function which is of central significance to life itself. Thomas Ambrogi's paper on "Sacramental Reality, Sign, and Presence" (which is not for those who cater to light reading) is a summary of the book *Christ the Sacrament of the Encounter with God,* written by the Dutch Catholic theologian E. Schillebeeckx. The author approaches the subject in the context of epistemology—that is, by examining words, communication, and the processes by which persons analyze and articulate experience. I can't buy everything in it, but found it enormously stimulating when wrestling with the nature and function of sacraments.

In this analysis, reference is made to the scholastic notion "that sacraments are signs rather than physically present things. To speak of the Eucharist (or any sacrament) as a sign is to introduce a certain duality into our thinking. For example, Thomas Ambrogi goes on to point out the duality between *word* (as uttered sound) and *idea.* "When we speak or listen to others speaking, we use words without attending to the difference between the sound patterns and the thought which they communicate: we grasp both together in an indissoluble unity. We do not attend, in other words, to word-sound as such—as *sign,* conveying that which is not itself—but simply to the meaning it expresses. . . . At the level of *action,* we have unity—identity of sign and signified; at the level of *reflection,* we have duality—the recognition of sign as sign, that is, as somehow not simply the same as the reality it expresses. These two levels are psychologically distinct: to attend to words as sounds means that one will not hear language, but noise" (page 183, emphases added).

Words in four languages are cited, all of which mean horse. To little children they are just four different noises, but to language students they all mean the same animal. The same thing is true, for example, in art. When I *look at* a picture on the wall, the object is a variety of colored pigments called paint, but what I *see* may be a landscape or the face of a person. Both are distinct, but inseparable. This unity-in-duality, the link between physical things and mental perception of them is universal for the human race. Without it, persons could not develop or communicate, and societies could not exist.

Applying this unity-in-duality to the sacraments, it is stated that "the new relationship between God and man which Christ has brought about is expressed and made tangible in visible actions and concrete objects. The Christian believer by his faith 'dwells in' and uses such signs in a manner similar to the way all men use language to convey thought. . . . Physical signs are not themselves 'meanings,' and yet without them 'meanings' could not exist. For meaning to be actualized there must be the word; for grace to be actualized and rendered accessible to man's consciousness, there must be preaching and sacrament. The visible *form* of the sacrament is something 'other' than pure sacramental *reality*. That reality itself—transformed human existence, the dwelling of God with man—requires the visible form and calls it into being in order to actualize itself at a particular time and place" (page 183, emphases added).

It's Still a Matter of Faith

I find this way of relating signs to realities quite meaningful when I reflect upon my own experience. The nonphysical realities which I cherish most—love, loyalty, beauty, truth, integrity—are closely wedded to the physical signs and symbols which communicate them to me. I've already mentioned the kiss as an example. From this viewpoint, the next step does not seem altogether insuperable: ". . . Christian sacramentalism goes beyond a general psychological analysis of symbolism. The 'real presence' of Christ in the sacraments cannot be verified merely in terms of the description of symbolic activity suggested above. But the Church's faith in the reality of sacramental presence is not something added on to her faith in the Christ-event; it is simply her belief in the Incarnation, expressing itself in the domain of ritual action. If God in Christ has become one with man, then the sacraments *are* what they signify" (page 184).

The Affirmation Versus the Explanation

We are now getting more and more deeply involved in the discussion. If you would like to see how much of a workout theological discussion can give the mind, hang on; but if the going gets so technical it becomes futile, you might skip ahead to the subtitle "The Mystery Deepens." That will summarize the discussion and admit to a bit of futility in itself. We will begin with a good theological exercise of classifying. In his paper on "Sacramental Sign" in the Lutheran Confessions, Warren Quanbeck summarizes the dominating elements as (1) the centrality of the Word of God: (2) the communion-meal character of the sacrament, and (3) the stress on the unity of the "action" of the Supper.

With respect to the first element, he emphasizes the biblical concept of the Word of God as central to the reality and understanding of the Lord's Supper. "The Lord's Supper is a visible, dramatic form of the Word of God, rooting in its institution by Jesus Christ, receiving its authority and efficacy through the coming together of God's Word and the created things used in accordance with the institution and purpose of God. Through it God continues to speak, reminding men dramatically of his saving deed in Christ, who through the sacrament becomes effectually present among His people and gives them the benefits of His death and resurrection. . . . One effect of this has been to discourage theological speculation as to the way in which Christ is present in the sacrament. Since his presence is an act of God effected through His Word, it is not accessible to man's understanding or to his powers of observation" (pages 81–82).

On the second point, Quanbeck quotes Luther's insistence that the sacrament is above all a meal, a communion of the believer with Christ and with his fellow Christians. Because of this he insisted that the Supper be celebrated only when communicants were present and that Communion be administered in both kinds (bread and wine, in contrast to the traditional Roman Catholic practice of withholding the wine from the laity).

With respect to the liturgical unity of the sacrament, the *Formula of Concord* is quoted as stating: "In this context 'use' or 'action' does not primarily mean faith, or the oral eating alone, but the entire external and visible action of the Supper as ordained by Christ. . . . Apart from this use it is not to be deemed a sacrament" (page 83). Quanbeck adds that the *Formula* uses the term *sign* both of the total sacramental action and of the elements of bread and wine.

Pressed by their opponents, Lutherans did develop theological definitions about the various manners or modes of Christ's presence. The *Formula of Concord* quotes Luther as listing three (Luther adds that there may be many more!), and also Luther's almost plaintive exclamation: "But who can explain or even conceive how this occurs? . . . it transcends nature and reason." Quanbeck also mentions another analogy, that of the presence of the *Logos* (Word) in the man Jesus. "Just as in Jesus Christ the two natures coexist without either nature being absorbed or changed into the other, so in the sacrament the body and blood of Christ are *under, with* and *in* the bread and wine. The reformers note that there is a significant difference: the union of the two natures in the person of Christ is a *personal* union; that of the body and blood of Christ with bread and wine is a *sacramental* union'' (page 87).

When Is a Mystery Not a Mystery?

After summarizing the explanation of transubstantiation given by the Council of Trent, Ambrogi comments, ''As theological explications of the limits of the mystery, these theories as they have been historically elaborated might well seem to be blasphemous sophistry, rationalistic attempts to contain the *mysterium tremendum* in explainable formulas. But theology need not necessarily be sophistry, and the Catholic theologian is somewhat nonplussed by a Lutheran's strong affirmation of the 'real presence' of Christ and then his absolute refusal to discuss theologically the nature of that presence or the manner in which a change is effected in the elements'' (page 162).

This reminds me of a remark once made by Roswell Barnes (about whom I spoke) when we were discussing the sad fact that he and I could not kneel side-by-side at Holy Communion, Lutherans and Presbyterians not being in formal church fellowship. ''I believe in Christ's real presence in the sacrament as much as you do,'' he said. ''The trouble is that you Lutherans say that the manner of this presence is a mystery, and then, darn it, you insist upon attaching a formula to it such as 'in, with, and under the elements.' That tells me very little. Why aren't you content to let a mystery remain a mystery?''

I had no pat answer, and still don't. Knutson writes: ''The Lutheran phraseology of 'in, with, and under' is easily misunderstood. Rather than limiting his presence, it seeks to characterize his presence as non-spatial . . . in a dynamic sense of being present in the whole activity of the sacrament as well as imparted by means of bread and wine'' (page 178). This does not destroy the mystery, but does add mysterious words. If you find a ''non-spatial presence'' hard to conceptualize, you have lots of company! To say what a thing is *not* is useful, but may not be much help in stating what it *is*.

More About Words

Words are indispensible, but have their limitations. Some years ago, there was a lot of literature written about the God-is-Dead school of theology. Critics of that slogan reply that if it means that God does not *exist,* it is right! The term *exist* is properly used only when dealing with finite things. A tree exists, as do people, and everything else in the natural world. But God as infinite cannot be said to exist as though he were in the same class as finite objects. The most that can be said within the limitations of human language to describe something outside of the natural world is to affirm that it is real. But applying this word in so limited a fashion in no way describes or explains that reality. The minute we begin explaining it, we slide over into the realm of faith. (The same is true of those who say that God is not real.)

Thus the words "sacramental presence" simply indicate a unique manner in which Christ's promise is fulfilled when his command is obeyed. We cannot explain it, but we accept and receive him in faith. Theological explications may be helpful in making us more sensitive to the reality of the experience, but cannot claim to be more than what they are: theological suggestions.

The Mystery Deepens

Turning now to what the joint summary statement says about "presence," the first paragraph lists the many ways through which Christ is among us in the world (page 192). The second paragraph affirms that "in the sacrament of the Lord's Supper Jesus Christ, true God and true man, is present wholly and entirely, in his body and blood, under the signs of bread and wine." This statement needs examination, especially the words "wholly and entirely."

Lutherans have tried to explain it in the past with the result that the mystery of the doctrine of the Trinity becomes even more mysterious, if such a thing is possible. Knutson sets forth the teachings of the Lutheran Confessions in the following words: "He comes to us as both God and man *from* his exalted state. . . . These doctrines teach that the divine attributes of the risen Lord are communicated to the human nature of the risen Lord without destroying or transforming the human nature. The human nature is thus able to be omnipresent. (Theologically described as *ubiquity*.) Whether this language is any longer viable for a modern man is debatable but its intention is clear. The Christ who is present is the 'whole' Christ, not the Lord as Spirit only, or divine nature only. Christ comes to man where man is with the promise that in this activity—through eating and drinking—he gives to us his body and blood: that is, himself, his life, and being. In saying this, Lutherans separate themselves from the Zwinglian tradition . . ." (page 177, brackets added). Zwingli had opposed Luther by arguing that since the risen Christ is seated at the right hand of God in heaven, he could not possibly be present in his human nature everywhere at Holy Communion. It should be added that the traditional Lutheran theological theory of ubiquity, while different from the Roman Catholic view of transubstantiation, was intended, like the latter, to make sense out of the reality of Christ's "sacramental presence." The Lutherans too had their theories.

At this point you may be ready to throw up your hands in despair about the whole business! To be candid, I have such moments: it seems so futile to attempt to unscrew the inscrutable. My mind boggles over the idea of the Trinity by itself; to add to this puzzle the notion that the second of the *three* persons in this *one* Godhead now possesses an omnipresent human nature not shared with the other two in an "undivided unity," is to leave me—from a human standpoint—completely baffled. It is understandable, then, why contemporary Lutheran theologians have abandoned attempts to explain the real presence. But I must keep in mind that such lack of clear understanding is not unique. The existence of the universe itself has no rational explanation. To describe it, however scientific the description may be, is not to explain it. We simply become aware of existence, accept it as given, and go on from there. A seminary professor once said to me: "My finite mind is incapable of understanding the infinite. That is why God became incarnate in Jesus Christ, and all I can know about God is what I see in Jesus." To be sure, the Scriptures have much to say about God, but always in anthropological (human) terms, such as walking in the Garden of Eden, seated on a throne, speaking the language of his listeners, subject to moods of love, wrath, and mercy. How else could one speak of him (or her or it)? To be sure we are told that God is infinite, eternal, all-knowing, omnipotent, present everywhere without being confined to any local point in space; but these words have meaning only by being the opposites of words we do understand. The Word of God must lead me into the realms of faith. Apart from that, there is no Christian understanding of life at all. If I refused to function because I can't explain why my heart beats, I wouldn't live very long!

To Put It in the Words of the Common Statement . . .

The third paragraph of the summary statement simply says: "Through the centuries Christians have attempted various formulations to describe this presence. . . . This manner of presence 'we can scarcely express in words' but we affirm his presence because we believe in the power of God and the promise of Jesus Christ, 'This is my body. . . . This is my blood. . . .' Our traditions have spoken of this presence as 'sacramental,' 'supernatural,' and 'spiritual.' [See the footnote: ". . . it is clear that *spiritual* here is not opposed to *real*."] These terms have different connotations in the two traditions, but they have in common a rejection . . . of an understanding of the sacrament as only commemorative or figurative. . . . The Lord's Supper is an effective sign: it communicates what it promises" (pages 192–193).

An Unresolved Difference

Having said this, the group remained divided on the question of whether or not the presence of Christ abides with the bread and wine remaining after the eucharistic celebration has ended. Roman Catholics, who see to it that all of the consecrated wine is consumed at the proper point in the Mass, believe that Christ's presence under the appearance of bread remains until the consecrated bread is eaten. That is why they reserve the bread as an object to be treated with reverence and even worship. Contemporary Roman Catholic theology stresses an important distinction on this point: it says that the host (bread) was originally reserved for communing the sick. That is still the primary purpose. "The adoration of Christ present in the reserved sacrament is of later origin and is a secondary end" (page 194). But the doctrine of the enduring presence has not changed. The Dutch *Catechism* referred to previously answers what it styles a "small question" as follows: "When does the eucharistic presence of Jesus cease? It ceases when the form of bread is no longer there."

I recall parts of the discussion vividly. Lutherans were asked whether bread and wine remaining from a service of Holy Communion are reconsecrated when used at a subsequent service. The answer was given that there is no fixed rule; the practices of pastors vary on this point. To which the next question was: "If it is necessary to reconsecrate the elements for another service, at what point did Christ leave?'' The very question reveals a gulf in the thinking of the two traditions on this subject. One Lutheran participant replied that the question was irrelevant. ''For us the Lord's Supper is a liturgical rite at the service of worship. Christ has invited us to be present and has promised that we will receive him under the forms of bread and wine. We come, do as he commanded, and he fulfills his promise. When the supper is over, it's over! In this context, the question of continuing presence is meaningless.'' Obviously Lutherans and Roman Catholics continue to disagree here.

(If you want to see how complicated this whole business can get, read Piepkorn's paper which compiles recent historical surveys on the subject (page 125). Theories vary and all too often they are contradicted by practice anyway. Thus, for example, he cites an instance in Wittenberg when a woman bumped the chalice as she was kneeling, spilling some of the wine on her clothing. After the service, Luther had the affected portion of her clothing cut out and burned, along with the wood that had been shaved from the choir stall on which the wine had splashed. ''Non-spatial'' presence? Could be, but people may get confused!)

Are the Remaining Disagreements Divisive?

But how important is this disagreement? Must we let it divide us? It is my strong conviction that here again the distinction between *church dogmas* (or doctrines) and *theological explications* should be made. The dogma is the fact of the presence and of its reception. The joint statement of the dialogue group affirms: ''Today, however, when Lutheran theologians read contemporary Catholic expositions, it becomes clear to them that the dogma of transubstantiation intends to affirm the fact of Christ's presence and of the change which takes place, and is not an attempt to explain *how* Christ becomes present'' (page 196, emphases added). This would seem to imply that the question regarding the precise time of the beginning and of the ending of this presence falls in the realm of theological opinion rather than that of dogma. The theological opinion in each tradition in no way denies the central dogma which affirms Christ's presence at the Lord's Supper. Cannot each respect the position of the other without adopting it, while clinging to fellowship in the apostolic faith?

The question is how much must we agree on before we commune together. Since this crucial question will come up repeatedly we should cite some sentences from McSorley's paper: "Christians are not in full communion when they disagree on binding dogmas of faith. It is one of the tasks of the ecumenical theological dialogue to overcome such *dogmatic disunity* between Churches. But this is not to say that *theological unity* must be sought. A variety of theologies can legitimately be developed within the one confession of faith. Consequently, when the ecumenical theologian finds himself in disagreement with a theologian of another tradition, he must ask himself: is his theological affirmation clearly incompatible with my Church's confession of faith, or can it be embraced as a legitimate theological viewpoint within the catholic unity of the Church? . . . [Karl] Rahner, whom no one has accused of failing to see theological differences, suggests 'that a too neurotic fear of being perhaps *really* in agreement *in depth* could disrupt the unity which is possible. Such fears . . . then give rise to those strange efforts . . . to find new sets of ever more subtle formulae and nuances so as to prove the existence of mutual dissent. . . . To have the right to live in separate Churches, one would have to be sure . . . that one is clearly in disagreement about the truth. It is not enough to be quite sure of being really in agreement, or of what the other exactly means or of having understood him quite correctly" (pages 24–25).

Searching for the Words that Best Express Our Faith

It is clear that on this subject, development of doctrine is continuing. Not many Lutherans are comfortable with Luther's declaration that in the Lord's Supper one "chews" Christ's body (even non-spatially). The search for analogies goes on. One gets a similar impression from the Dutch *New Catechism* when it states that "This is a mysterious presence. We must not imagine, for instance, that Christ's body enters our mouth in a very small edition, so to speak, just as in Nazareth he entered the house of Mary in actual life size. . . . It is better to say that the bread is essentially withdrawn from its normal human meaning or definition, and has become the bread which the Father has given us, Jesus himself" (page 343).

The dialogue group did not attempt to cover the entire doctrine of the Eucharist, but only the two aspects of it (sacrifice and presence) which have been the most divisive. The convergence of views among those taking part is quite evident, but this does not mean that the churches represented have gone that far in their pilgrimage toward unity. My eye caught a striking question in McCue's paper (page 113) where he indicated that Luther never regarded the *how* question of Christ's presence in the Lord's Supper to be very important; that it was the very *triviality* of the theory of transubstantiation which made its *dogmatization* so very important. "In posing the problem as he does, he (Luther) brings to the surface a problem. . . . Is it a legitimate exercise of papal or conciliar authority to define as true . . . a proposition which is admittedly not required by scripture or reason, and which seems to make no difference whatsoever to anything?" We can be affirmed to know these thinkers try to be careful not to let technicality sink to triviality. That distinction is not always easily made. Our whole understanding of the faith could turn on one technicality while being unaffected by another.

I identify myself completely with the conclusion of the dialogue group: "Despite all remaining differences in the ways we speak and think of the eucharistic sacrifice and our Lord's presence in his supper, we are no longer able to regard ourselves as divided in the one holy catholic and apostolic faith on these two points. We therefore prayerfully ask our fellow Lutherans and Catholics to examine their consciences and root out many ways of thinking, speaking, and acting, both individually and as churches, which has obscured their unity in Christ on these and many other matters."

Of course there are unanswered questions. There always will be. It's inherent in the human condition to "see through a glass darkly," as St. Paul observed. But with all our limitations we can and must probe in faith where knowledge falls short. I never forget the charge of a Reformed churchman who once said to me: "Paul, you don't celebrate the Lord's Supper; you celebrate the Lutherans' Supper!" I fear that to some extent this can be said of all Christian communions to the extent that they identify the development of *their* understandings of Christ's institution of this "sacrament" with *his* intention in an absolute way. Our wrestling with these subjects has drawn us into the profound depths of the mysteries of life itself. Fortunate indeed are those who can hold knowledge and faith in creative tension while being able to distinguish clearly between them.

Dilemmas for discussion:

1. How do sacraments bring us the real thing?
2. How are we saved? (explained in terms of atonement, forgiveness, reconciliation, rebirth in the spirit, liberation)
3. How can the explainable words of the liturgy express the inexplainable mysteries of life?
4. What do we think, feel, or do when we "receive Christ" in the sacrament?

DISCUSSION

Suggestions for a Discussion of the Eucharist

- You could present this case study for discussion:

  Marie had grown up in the Roman Catholic Church. Her husband Lou had grown up in the Lutheran church. They were at a military outpost and both went to worship services everytime a chaplain visited the post, whether the chaplain was Protestant or Catholic.
  When the Catholic priest led the services, Marie would genuflect as she entered the chapel. Lou asked why. She explained that she was giving reverence to the Christ in the Eucharist host. She asked if Lou didn't believe that Christ was really present. He responded that he had been taught that the bread remained bread.
  What was the difference in their beliefs? What was the similarity?

- Various participants could use their own words to summarize their understanding of the Christian faith. As the understandings are given, write some of the key words you hear used on the chalkboard. If both Catholics and Lutherans are present, put the key words used by the Catholics on one side of the board and the key words used by Lutherans on the other side. After this is completed, go through the words. Check which words are identical or have similar meaning, and which are different. A check could also be made on what the words mean to the participants. They might have different meanings.

- After the key words have been placed on the chalkboard, go over them. Try to see which ones have some kind of relation to the Eucharist, Holy Communion. Circle those that are especially expressed in Communion. After this, go through the circled words and put a cross mark beside those that emphasize the sacrifice of Christ. Are more words crossed than not? (If members of both groups are represented, how do the number of words associated with Catholics compare with the number of words associated with Lutherans?)

The point of this exercise is to check how the subject of the sacrifice comes out in the discussion. The sacrifice is emphasized in both churches and is represented in a number of ways.

CHAPTER 4

Eucharist and Ministry

The dialogue participants were surprised to find that they agreed on so many issues regarding the Eucharist. They were surprised because historically the issues had been so divisive. Because of their discoveries of agreement they were eager to plunge immediately into the subject of intercommunion—may Lutherans and Roman Catholics commune together? The next meeting focused upon this topic, but a major obstacle soon came into view. That was the question of who is to administer the sacrament. The issue was the validity of the Ministry presiding over the celebration of the Eucharist. There had been a hint of this in the discussion on Baptism, when (as I vividly recall) a Lutheran asked our Roman Catholic colleagues, "If you accept our Baptism as valid and thus that we are together with you in the Body of Christ, why shouldn't we be welcomed to join you in the Lord's Supper?" There was a pause, after which the response was: "We really hadn't thought of it, but if we invited you, would you come?" The half-jesting reply to that question was: "Probably not, but we think you should invite us anyway!"

An Outline of the Issue

Lutherans and Roman Catholics (also Eastern Orthodox and Anglicans) agree on the biblical testimony that Christ established a Ministry, usually called apostolic, to lead the church in fulfilling the various aspects of its mission until he should return in glory. (In the joint statement, this Ministry is designated by the uppercase "M" to distinguish it from the ministry of the whole church or people of God. This doesn't imply a higher status, but rather a particular function; cf. 1 Corinthians 12:28: "God has appointed in the church first apostles, second prophets . . ." The study papers do not use this device of capitals and lowercase.)

So far, so good. The apostles, including the Twelve and others such as Paul—no one knows just how many—were known, and their authority was generally accepted. Precisely how this leadership functioned is not spelled out in the New Testament. One might surmise that Christ's second coming was regarded as so near, that long-range planning regarding church order was a marginal concern. But as the years went by and the original apostles were executed, or died naturally, the question of the continuation of their authority had to be determined. Subsequent patterns were not uniform, and documented evidence is often ambiguous or fuzzy. So here enters the element of the development of doctrine described in the chapter on Baptism. New Testament descriptions of life in the early church do not draw clear lines between functions of bishops and presbyters (priests). By the time of the second century, the office of bishop seems to have been accorded the greater weight of authority in most places. The Roman Catholic Church taught that this trend was the work of the Holy Spirit.

From this basis, the Roman Catholic Church regards as valid Ministers only those who have been ordained by bishops consecrated by the laying on of hands in an unbroken line of apostolic episcopal succession. Orthodox priests qualify; Lutheran pastors presumably do not. (Anglican priests and Swedish pastors may meet this criterion because of the way they have been ordained, but their ministry raises a different aspect of the problem which we will not cover here.) Since one of the functions of priests is to preside over the celebration of the Eucharist, and since Lutheran pastors have not been regarded as valid Ministers by Roman Catholic standards, it would seem to follow that according to such criteria, no celebration of the Lord's Supper in Lutheran churches is or has been valid. Intercommunion is therefore impossible.

The Lutheran Counterposition

This issue of ministry has been the major roadblock to reconciliation between our two communions in the twentieth century. The issue has been more of a roadblock than the traditional disputes regarding Scripture versus tradition or justification by grace through faith, though of course there are implications in the doctrine of the ministry related to these two issues. Lutherans insist that the only true apostolic succession is that of the *apostolic faith* passed down from generation to generation with "the Gospel rightly taught and the Sacraments rightly administered" (*The Augsburg Confession,* Article VII). The gospel authenticates the minister, not vice versa. The two positions at first glance seem irreconcilable, similar to an irresistible force meeting an immovable object.

A Meeting Ground

Happily, such need not be the case, as the documents published in the booklet entitled *Eucharist and Ministry* indicate. Again, a major factor at work has been Vatican II which, while not reversing earlier positions, spawned wider interpretations. The joint statement of the dialogue group is deliberately cautious and limited in what it asserts. It provides some historical and biblical background, describes the respective traditions for structuring the Ministry, and concludes: "*These ways in which the Ministry has been structured and implemented in our two traditions appear to us to be consonant with apostolic teaching and practice.* We are agreed that the basic reality of the apostolic Ministry can be preserved amid *variations* in structure and implementation, in rites of ordination, and in theological explanation. As we learn more of the complex history of the Ministry, we begin to grasp the ways in which this gift of God to his church is able to assimilate valuable elements from different ages and cultures without losing its authentic apostolic character. In this context we find that the present moment speaks persuasively to us, urging both the renewal of what is basic in our apostolic heritage as well as openness to the variants that our Christian witness to the world requires . . . we are aware of the difficulties implied therein for both of our traditions. . . . That we have not found these difficulties insuperable is indicated by the recommendations which each group has been able to make" (pages 15–16, emphases added).

Nothing is said here yet about intercommunion, but plenty is being said if the words are given full weight. We see that as we read the separate group recommendations.

The Separate Interpretative Statements

The joint statement conclusion is followed by two sections entitled "Reflections," in which the Lutheran participants and the Roman Catholic participants respectively make additional observations from the standpoint of the two traditions. In effect, each ground addresses its own constituency to explain how and why it could concur in a statement regarding the Ministry which goes considerably beyond any position previously taken on either side. Formerly such comments had been made by individuals, for example, by Knutsen and McSorley in assessing the statement on *Eucharist as Sacrifice*. In that instance, the more difficult task fell to the Lutherans, for prejudices regarding the subject have been very deep over four centuries and are not easily dislodged. In dealing with the Ministry, however, the burden fell mostly on the Roman Catholics; for while the Lutheran Confessions nowhere deny the validity of Roman Catholic ordination, the Council of Trent was generally regarded as stating emphatically that priests or pastors nor ordained by a bishop in apostolic succession were not valid ministers of the church. (For more on this point, refer to the paper on Trent by McSorley, with which not all of the Roman Catholic participants were in agreement.)

Lutheran Reservations and Affirmations

These separate statements too are very cautious. The Lutherans state many positive things about Eucharist and Ministry in the Roman Catholic Church, but then add: "Although we see our common statement as removing some of the obstacles that separate Roman Catholics and Lutherans, there are still problems to be discussed before we can recommend pulpit and altar fellowship" (pages 21–22). Some of these are mentioned in a footnote to the common statement: ". . . the apostolic Ministry and succession of the bishop of Rome and its relationship to the apostleship of Peter and Paul; infallibility, especially as applied to papal infallibility; the distinction between matters that are of divine law and those which are of human law . . . ; the question of a purely charismatic ministry; questions of eucharistic sharing; the specific relations of a presbyterally ordained Ministry to an episcopally oriented Ministry; and, finally, the practical problems of mutual recognition of Ministries, including psychological, canonical, and administrative factors" (page 15). Quite a formidable list! Some of them were dealt with later in the discussions on papal primacy and infallibility. I am happy to report that a lot of progress has been made in the years since 1970 when this statement was issued.

The nub of the Lutheran reflections is found in the final paragraph (page 22):

"As Lutherans, we joyfully witness that in theological dialogue with our Roman Catholic partners we have again seen clearly a fidelity to the proclamation of the Gospel and the administration of the sacraments which confirms our historic conviction that the Roman Catholic Church is an authentic church of our Lord Jesus Christ. For this reason we recommend to those who have appointed us that through appropriate channels the participating Lutheran churches be urged to declare formally their judgment that the ordained Ministers of the Roman Catholic Church are engaged in a valid Ministry of the Gospel, announcing the Gospel of Christ and administering the sacraments of faith as their chief responsibilities, and that the body and blood of our Lord Jesus Christ are truly present in their celebrations of the sacrament of the altar."

Roman Catholic Affirmations . . .

The Roman Catholic statements entitled *Reflections* start out by saying that in the course of the dialogue, "our traditional objections to the Lutheran eucharistic Ministry were seen to be of less force today, and reasons emerged for a positive reappraisal." They too go into the historical evidence of the apostolic and early generations of Christian communities. Regarding this, they state: "By way of summation, we find from the historical evidence that by the sixteenth century there had been a long and almost exclusive practice whereby the only Minister of the eucharist was one ordained by a bishop who had been consecrated as heir to a chain of episcopal predecessors. Yet, in this long history there are lacunae [that is, points where evidence is lacking], along with exceptions that offer some precedent for the practice adopted by the Lutherans" (page 25).

They then proceed to the "Theological Arguments," stating at the beginning that "as we Catholic participants in the dialogue examined the difficulties, we found that they no longer seemed insuperable" (pages 26). The theological problems are then taken one by one and generally seen either no longer to exist or as not insurmountable with appropriate qualifications noted. Their conclusion (pages 31–32) is: "As Roman Catholic theologians, we acknowledge in the spirit of Vatican II that the Lutheran communities with which we have been in dialogue are truly Christian churches, possessing the elements of holiness and truth that mark them as organs of grace and salvation. Furthermore, in our study we have found serious defects in the arguments customarily used against the validity of the eucharistic Ministry of the Lutheran churches. In fact, we see no persuasive reason to deny the possibility of the Roman Catholic Church recognizing the validity of this Ministry. Accordingly, we ask the authorities of the Roman Catholic Church whether the ecumenical urgency flowing from Christ's will for unity may not dictate that the Roman Catholic Church recognize the validity of the Lutheran Ministry and, correspondingly, the presence of the body and blood of Christ in the eucharistic celebrations of the Lutheran churches."

. . . and Stipulations

In the perspective of past controversies, this statement by Roman Catholics was rightly described as a breakthrough. The carefully chosen language of the recommendations contained limitations; and, lest those be overlooked, the final five paragraphs add clarifications which are extremely important. The statement focuses upon *present* teachings and practices without dealing with past situations. *Church* action is called for which should precede private practice; the view expressed is restricted to the Lutheran churches which have been thus studied; the recommendation does not automatically imply intercommunion, since there are remaining problems. Two comments merit full quotation: "Nor do we attempt to decide whether recognition by the Roman Catholic Church would be constitutive of validity or merely confirmatory of existing validity." (This has been singled out by critics as a serious reservation.) The reservation is spelled out: "In speaking of the recognition of a Lutheran Ministry not ordained by bishops, we are not in any way challenging the age-old insistence on ordination by a bishop within our own church or covertly suggesting that it be changed. While we believe that the church of Jesus Christ is free to adapt the structure of the divinely instituted Ministry in the way she sees fit (so long as the essential meaning and function of apostolic Ministry is retained), we affirm explicitly that the apostolic Ministry is retained in a preeminent way in the episcopate, the presbyterate, and the diaconate. We would rejoice if episcopacy in apostolic succession, functioning as the effective sign of church unity, were acceptable to all; but we have envisaged a practical and immediate solution in a *de facto* situation where episcopacy is not yet seen in that light'' (pages 32–33).

The Study and Dialogue Process

That is how the discussion came out. How did they arrive there? As usual, the group began with the biblical study, searching for light on the subject from the New Testament. Jerome Quinn's paper is a scholarly but extremely readable treatment. Although a wide array of details about activities and problems in the first generation churches can be gathered from Acts of the Apostles and other New Testament books, no clear and consistent pattern of church order can be drawn from them. There is no doubt that the Twelve had a special authority and leadership role. When the vacancy created by Judas' defection was filled, Matthias was chosen probably from several who met the criteria of (1) having been with Jesus together with the original Twelve from the beginning, and (2) having witnessed the Resurrection. (An interesting sidelight is that although several women are given prominent roles in the New Testament, they are excluded from consideration as apostles, apparently because in the Jewish world of that time they were unable to give legally acceptable evidence—yet, in the Gospel accounts, women were the first to see the risen Lord!)

Thus an unknown number of men who were with Jesus before and after the Resurrection were commissioned by him and described as apostles, including but not limited to the Twelve. Paul claimed to be an apostle on the basis of his encounter with Jesus on the road to Damascus. (See McCue, page 143.)

As the church grew and problems arose, the Twelve appointed seven men ''of good repute, full of the Spirit and of wisdom" to take charge of daily distribution at the tables. . . . This would relieve the Twelve to devote themselves to "prayer and the ministry of the word" (Acts 6:1-4). But Quinn notes that "it is striking that the Seven are never depicted as exercising the function for which they were chosen. Instead they exercise a form of ministry . . . which the Twelve had reserved when they appointed the Seven" (pages 84-85). Both Stephen and Philip are reported engaged in preaching. Later on, the category of presbyters or elders appears, both in Jerusalem and in the churches founded by Paul. After looking at all the references, Quinn comments that the Pastoral Epistles "demand practically the same qualifications for an *episkopos* [bishop] as for the *presbyteroi* [presbyters], and the latter appear to share in the functions of an *episkopos*" (page 97, brackets added). For purposes of comparison, we would consider a presbyter the equivalent of a priest or pastor.

Varieties in Practice

Thus is it certain that the apostolic role was passed on, traditionally accompanied by the laying on of hands by one or more possessing that status. But speaking of the generation after the fall of Jerusalem, Quinn remarks: "It is notable that even in this period the New Testament documents do not explictly name those who conducted the eucharist . . . It is distinctly possible that in the oldest Jewish-Christian churches the Ministry of prophets and teachers included leading the eucharist whereas in the mixed congregations the *presbyteroi-episkopoi* eventually emerged with this function" (page 98).

Duchaine records that, at the first meeting on this subject, the biblical scholars presented a list of six points upon which they were in agreement, which can be summarized as follows: The first churches planted by Christian leaders included persons charged with authority; these patterns of leadership varied; the term *apostle* can be viewed as functional, but apostles were not tied to a local church; "The seven" in the Book of Acts carry out the same functions as the twelve apostles in Acts; ministry is something committed to the entire church; because of the variety in the structure of the early Christian churches, the presiding official in the church's ministry at eucharistic celebrations varied (page 35).

In view of this variety, how can the New Testament help in determining the criteria for a valid Ministry? John Reumann suggested that the New Testament cannot be brought up into the twentieth century apart from consideration of intervening centuries of history and development, but "it still does provide some norms and guidance for current questions" (page 36).

Continuing Development

When one begins to examine the evidence from the "intervening centuries" found in the writings which were excluded from the New Testament canon (some of which are copied in ancient manuscripts along with biblical books and which are printed in the New Testament Apocrypha) it appears that variations in practice with respect to the structure and function of the Ministry continued to be widespread. James McCue's interesting account contains many citations from which it may be inferred that there were presbyters and others outside of episcopal succession who functioned in the Ministry without the validity of this being questioned. There were exceptions and loopholes which can be pounced upon as precedents by those arguing for a valid Ministry through presbyteral succession. The issue seems to have emerged at the time when doctrinal controversies threatened the faith. The Gnostics were a great threat. They taught that Christ was not human—he only seemed to be. They believed he was God's divine creation sent into an evil, material world to liberate persons through his special relations. They denied a) the infallibility of the apostles, b) the apostolicity, or at least the exclusive apostolicity, of the church's Scriptures, and/or c) the correctness of the church's interpretation of those Scriptures.

Here we are seeing that we cannot escape the question of what authority the apostles had. History has too much experience with that question to allow us to ignore it.

Irenaeus was one of the leading early church fathers who fought the Gnostic heresy. His position is summed up by McCue as follows: "He [Irenaeus] simply assumes that the apostles were fully enlightened with the coming of the Holy Spirit; and on this assumption he argues that the apostles would not have held back the more important parts of the gospel from those to whom they publicly entrusted the guidance of the churches. Hence one can look about today and see who those are who have been the recipients, *per successiones* [through succession] of the apostolic tradition. These apostolic bishops and apostolic churches can serve as norms in determining which are the genuinely apostolic books and what is the truly apostolic faith" (pages 158–159, brackets added).

Apostolic Churches as the Norm

McCue adds: "Irenaeus does not seem to require an apostolic pedigree for the existence of the church; at least he nowhere says that this is necessary. That is, a church not established by an apostle is validated according to the Irenaean scheme of things not (or at least not primarily) through a succession of ordinations going back to an apostle. It is validated by being in agreement and harmony with the norm churches, those of apostolic foundation and public episcopal succession.

"In Irenaeus' conception the apostolic church . . . is more central than the idea of conferral of power from one bishop to another through episcopal consecration or ordination" (page 159).

McCue, in mentioning the early "episcopal succession lists" composed about the middle of the second century, says that they "have generated a good bit of skepticism." He comments that in Irenaeus' time, "Election by the people and their presence along with the presbyterate are also a part of this liturgy [ordination], and there is no reason to suppose that these were just the trimmings . . . we might say that one becomes a successor to the apostles through ordination for an apostolic church rather than simply through ordination by any bishop whatsoever; and thus the 'bearer' of apostolicity in the ordination rite is the church—that is, the people and the presbyterate—rather than the participating bishops" (page 160, brackets added). Again, "Thus, though certain expressions may seem to lend support to later absolutizing tendencies, for these earlier writers, apostolic succession 'guarantees' nothing" (page 161).

Succession in the Orthodox Faith

Tertullian, in about the same period, is cited as declaring that "the emphasis does not fall on a quasi-physical transmission *via* ordination of apostolic-episcopal power and authority. It is the handing-on of the orthodox faith that is crucial" (page 162). "We are therefore led to suppose, at the very least, that Tertullian took it for granted that a quite proper eucharist could take place, in case of necessity, without ordination of the celebrant by a bishop standing in apostolic succession'' (page 163). Clement of Alexandria is quote as stressing the central role of the succession of doctrine rather than a succession of bishops. Also, McCue notes that "the church in Alexandria (and Egypt) apparently did not use the same episcopal ordination practices that we find in other places. At least down through the time of Origen, the bishop of Alexandria seems to have been chosen and consecrated by the presbyters of that city'' (pages 167–168).

A Trend Seen in Perspective

Many other instances of differing practices in the first two or three centuries can be cited to illustrate the variety of valid ministries in those times.

In all fairness, even as these quotations should be read in context so that particular circumstances in each instance are noted, just so they must be seen in the perspective of the general trend. Walter Burghardt describes the trend by seven "moments.'' He is numbering different aspects of succession to the apostles suggested or stressed by different writers, in different periods, at different places (pages 173–177). These can be summarized as follows:

1. There was in the early years a succession of *principle.* For Clement of Rome (about A.D. 96) men personally ordained by the apostles were to be succeeded by other men approved and appointed by other reputable men with the consent of the whole church. . . . This is not a succession to apostleship (for Clement, the apostolate as a distinct office passed away with the original apostles); it is a succession to the *episkope* which the apostles exercised.
2. Then came the succession in *office.* . . . The interplay here is important. On the one hand, the argument is that the persons who held the office taught the truth because they were who they were. On the other hand, they would not have been who they were if they were not teaching two doctrines. *Without orthodox doctrine, succession ceases or never really begins*; bishops are in the true succession insofar as they teach the true doctrine.
3. Next came the succession of *doctrine.* Here we confront a line of teachers who have received and transmitted apostolic doctrine with Christian fidelity.

4. A fourth moment came in succession of *authority, power,* and *jurisdiction.* It comes by evolution early in the third century. In the first place, authority, power, jurisdiction is claimed in connection with apostolic succession. . . . In the second place, whereas for Irenaeus, Hegesippus, and Tertullian, "bishops have their place in the apostolic succession only in connection with the churches over which they preside," with Hippolytus, perhaps for the first time, "succession from the apostles seems to be a personal possession of the bishop. . . . For the first time, apparently, the bishops are not merely in succession from the apostles, but they themselves are *successors* of the apostles" (quoted from C. H. Turner, *Apostolic Succession*). In the third place the Hippolytean idea in the evolution of apostolic succession comes to full flower in Cyprian, with whom . . . the apostolate *is* the episcopate.
5. There is, fifth, the succession of *history.* This approach to apostolic succession is not from a doctrinal or sacramental, but from an almost exclusively *historical* perspective. It involves a heavily juridical view of succession: an office is ultimately justified because it can be traced back to the apostles.
6. There is, sixth, the succession in *disunity.* It comes with the whole agonizing conflict over the validity of orders conferred *outside the unity* of the church. For example, reordination was demanded by Cyprian, but not by Augustine.
7. There is, last, the succession of *bishop.* After Cyprian, surely with the fourth century, the idea of bishop (in distinction from presbyter) as successor to the apostles in *leitourgia* (the Christian ministry) became quite the common thing. Not that the bishop inherits apostleship; he is not simply identifiable with the apostles. Rather that, in the minds of the fathers at least, the bishop, like the apostle, represents within his community the unity of the church, is the primary guardian of the tradition of the apostles, and exercises jurisdiction (authoritative teaching, juridical action) after the fashion of the apostles.

The Elusive Normative

I have quoted at great length from these two study papers because they show how sparse the evidence from history is to explain the trend in the early centuries toward the episcopal supremacy which ultimately prevailed in the Roman Catholic Church. Burghardt's final paragraph is worth quoting in its entirety: "From the above, what is 'normative' here? What is binding on later ages? This is as difficult to answer as is the question, what is 'normative' for Christian ministry in the light of the New Testament evidence? Perhaps a restatement of the essential *fact* as I see it will be sufficient for our purposes in the present dialogue. In the first two centuries of patristic thought, great emphasis was laid on the need of being in the *doctrinal* succession of the apostles (fidelity to the gospel); for otherwise, one is not really a Christian. But this is not *simply* guaranteed by looking at the doctrine. There is a mutual interplay: doctrinal *integrity* and an identifiable *chain* (most often those in official position). Put another way: doctrinal communion and legitimate appointment. The *manner* of appointment is often difficult to determine—more difficult the farther back one goes. And, of course, still to be satisfactorily determined is the precise meaning of *episkopoi* and *presbyteroi* in the first two centuries—an issue of vital importance in the quest for the normative" (page 177).

Confrontation Culminating in the Reformation

Although cracks in the unity between the Eastern Orthodox churches and the Western churches which acknowledged the primacy of the bishop of Rome began in the year 589, and the Eastern Orthodox patriarch and the pope in Rome excommunicated each other in 1054, the evolution of the authority of the episcopal succession described above was not seriously questioned until the period which culminated in the sixteenth-century Reformation. There were many in the Roman Catholic Church pressing for reform. Some critics were excommunicated and their influence contained; or like John Hus, they were executed. That Martin Luther survived and the movement he initiated became widespread was due to complex political and social as well as ecclesiastical factors. In the initial stages of his protest, he did not question the authority of bishops and the pope, but rather urged the latter to insist upon the correction of what he regarded as theological errors and moral abuses tolerated by bishops of this time. As a result he was expelled from the church, and it is likely that only the protection of his political authorities saved him from being burned at the stake.

In that instance, excommunication failed to suppress the influence of a critic. The times were ripe for revolt, and Luther's voice had the effect of a match in a dry forest. His teachings spread over most of central Europe. Many groups who thought he did not go far enough started even more radical movements. Ultimately the counter-Reformation within the Roman Catholic Church took place, followed by bitter and bloody wars. In Scandinavia and Finland, led by both bishops and political authorities, the entire church followed the "evangelical" reform; and in Sweden today, pastors receive episcopal ordination in the same way as before. The pope refused to authorize episcopal ordination to priests (later called pastors) in those central European churches which adopted Luther's position. This led to a reexamination of the doctrine of the Ministry, going back to the scriptural evidence mentioned earlier in this chapter. The conclusions were written in the Lutheran Confessions and are summarized in Arthur Carl Piepkorn's study paper.

The Ministry in the Lutheran Confessions

The following points noted by Piepkorn are useful for our purposes. Without belittling the role of the universal priesthood of believers, the Confessions teach that the church has the responsibility of choosing, calling, and ordaining fit persons to carry out the church's responsibility of proclaiming the gospel and administering the sacraments. Only such persons are competent publicly and responsibly to proclaim the gospel and administer the sacraments. "The Gospel gives *those who rule over the churches* the command to teach the Gospel, to remit sins, and to administer the sacraments. . . . This authority by divine right is common to *all who rule over churches,* whether they are called pastors, presbyters, or bishops" (pages 103–104). Ordination by existing bishops is permissible for the sake of love and good order, but it is not necessary. The confessions do make reference to "the sacrament of orders," but in a lesser sense, not up to the level of Baptism and Holy Communion. Piepkorn adds that "Since this proclamation and application of the gospel and this administration of the sacraments is precisely the task of the sacred ministry, the sacred ministry itself becomes a 'mark' or characteristic of the church" (page 107).

In his study paper on "Ordained Minister and Layman in

Lutheranism," John Reumann summarizes the historic position as follows: "In the context of the priesthood of all believers and in order to proclaim the gospel, the Lutheran Reformation regards a functional ministry, instituted by God, as necessary in the church, a ministry of the office of the word, ordained normally by pastor-presbyter-bishops. Like the laity, this special ministry serves the gospel. Ministry and laity work reciprocally, but the ministry has functions which differentiate it from the general priesthood of the baptized (page 242).

The Council of Trent on the Ministry

The teachings of the Reformers were repudiated at the Council of Trent which was convened in 1545 and lasted with interruptions of three and ten years until 1563. The decisions of the council are examined by Harry McSorley in two study papers. Both give examples of the relationship between dogmas and doctrines or opinions, referred to earlier. A basic question is: "We know what the councils *said,* but what did they *mean*?" It should also be mentioned that there is general agreement that at Trent the bishops did not know precisely the theological position of the Reformers on this subject.

Not Valid or Not Authorized?

McSorley asks about the meaning of words. He asks, for example, about the meaning of the word *competent* in the Roman Catholic teaching of the "competent" minister of the Eucharist. Trent at many times defined the "orders" in the Ministry, according to how they are "valid," "legitimate," or "authorized." McSorley cites as the most relevant statement of Trent on this subject the condemnation of those who say that persons "who have neither been rightly ordained nor commissioned by ecclesiastical and canonical power, but come from elsewhere, are legitimate . . . ministers of the word and of the sacraments" (page 131). McSorley's question is: If the priest or pastor presiding over the Eucharist is not, according to Roman Catholic standards, validly or legitimately ordained and thus is not authorized (in its view) to do so, but otherwise administers the sacrament in an authentic fashion, is the sacrament itself nevertheless real and effective? Do the participants receive the body and blood of Christ? He construes Trent's use of the word "power" as possibly meaning "authority," that is, the sacrament cannot be administered without the church's permission. "The burden of Trent's teaching, then, is that those who are not ordained according to the canonical authority of the church . . . are not *legitimate* ministers of word and sacrament. Trent does not say that the word preached by illegitimately constituted ministers is a nonpreaching of the word, nor that the eucharist celebrated by such ministers is not the sacrament of the eucharist" (page 132).

Switching to my own language, this is like saying that an illegitimate baby is nonetheless a baby! Or an operation performed by a doctor not certified by public authorities is still an operation, and a car driven by a motorist who has no license goes somewhere nevertheless. Back to McSorley: "What *cannot* be concluded from Trent or claimed to be part of Trent's teaching, is that the 'power' that is handed on to the ministerial priests of the church in the sacrament of order (1) can be conferred in no other way except through the sacrament of order; (2) is so absolutely necessary for consecrating the eucharist that without it, regardless of circumstances, 'nothing happens' if one attempts to offer the eucharist" (page 288). Not all Roman Catholic participants accepted these interpretations of what Trent "meant" to say. Some were ready to concede that Vatican II opened the door a crack for such developments in that direction. As will be seen later, the implications of a council's teachings may leave room for a variety of interpretations.

The Contemporary Situation—Lutheran

So now we come to the present day. What is the situation at the moment? Warren Quanbeck summarizes the current Lutheran stance in his paper "A Contemporary View of Apostolic Succession." After referring to the Reformation background, and listing factors which are making possible a mutual reexamination of the issue, he asks the question: "What does apostolicity consist of, and how is it mediated in the life of the churches?" A stimulating reply is given in his brief account of an essay of Professor Edmund Schlink of Germany, compressed into eight points and a summary (pages 182–184). Quanbeck then gives his own views (pages 185–187) which contain the following statements:

1. "There is no continuation of the apostolic office in the

narrow sense . . . What continues in the church is the mission or service of the apostle. . . .

2. The leader in the church, like the apostle, stands over against the churches as representative of Jesus Christ. When he proclaims the apostolic gospel, it is Jesus Christ who speaks through him. . . .

3. The leader of the church, like the apostle, stands with all church members under the grace and judgment of God. His preeminence as leader does not mean exaltation or dominance but precisely the opposite. Nothing humbles as thoroughly as the call to the ministry. . . .

4. The leader of the church, like the apostle, is called to service in the fellowship of the congregation . . . the New Testatment does not distinguish as we do between the magisterium or the ministry of the word and the other ministries of the church. . . .

5. The leader of the church, like the apostle, works in the context of the charismatic gifts . . . the leader is not the only one with whom the Spirit has dealings. . . .

6. The leader of the church, like the apostle, is called to be a bond of unity in the church . . . Because of this concern for unity, the leader has a certain preeminence among the gifts of the Spirit. . . .

7. The office of leadership in the church, like that of the apostle whose mission and service it continues, is a complex combination . . . To grasp the full meaning of leadership in the church as apostolic succession one must grasp this rich dynamic complexity of calling and response, of tradition and traditioning of leadership in service, of life in the Spirit, of keeping unity in the bond of peace.

8. Since apostleship in the narrower sense is limited to the first generation Christians, apostolic succession means a following in the apostles' footsteps . . . This succession can be founded on a general call addressed to all baptized people, or on the special calling to the ministry of word and sacraments.

Apostolic succession in the narrower sense as succession through episcopal ordination is not a *sine qua non* [an indispensible] of the apostolic succession of church and ministry. It does not produce an apostolic succession and authority which are missing from other types of ordination. But ordination by episcopal imposition of hands should be seen as a sign of the apostolic succession of the ministry and of the church, and therefore a sign of the unity and catholicity of the church. Lutherans should for this reason acknowledge the usefulness of ordination by bishops through the history of the church as a sign of apostolicity . . . But the sign must never be separated from the reality which it signifies, namely, the apostolic tradition. The sign of apostolic succession cannot take away the necessity of a constantly renewed submission to the gospel as it is communicated in the apostolic tradition, nor can it devalue the pastoral ministry which exists without episcopal ordination'' (brackets added).

The Status of Other Ministries in the Church

I have quoted Warren Quanbeck rather extensively, for he states concisely the general Lutheran position on the Ministry. I should add, however, that there is considerable discussion going on in Lutheran churches about the role of the laity in the ministry of the whole church. An example is found in the book *Christianity and Real Life*, (Philadelphia: Fortress, 1976) written by William E. Diehl, a layperson who insists—rightly in my judgment—that the church has virtually ignored the ministries of lay persons in life outside the institutional church, and should give more support to such ministries.

Quanbeck does use the phrase ''a certain preeminence'' when relating the Ministry to gifts of the Spirit cited in 1 Corinthians 12, but this relates to the concern for unity. Perhaps the following example will bring out the point. As a parish pastor, each year I used the ''Order for the Installation of a Church Council'' to induct newly elected council members. After referring to the way in which the Twelve ''called the multitude of disciples unto them, and said, it is not reason that we should leave the word of God, and serve tables. Wherefore, brethren, look ye out among you seven men of honest report, full of the Holy Ghost and wisdom, whom we may appoint over this business.'' On page 288 of the *Common Service Book of the Lutheran Church* (The United Lutheran Church in America, 1917), the ''Order for the Installation of a Church Council'' lists the duties of the church council. The first one given is ''That the services of God's House be held at the proper times, and conducted in accordance with the Order of the Church; that the pure Word of God be preached, as the Church confesses it . . .'' (page 288). Good people as they were, there was not a single one of those council persons well enough versed to ascertain that all my words from the pulpit were indeed in accordance with the "pure Word of God." They simply assumed that a pastor ordained by the church had the competence and integrity to keep the preaching pure, and that their main job was finance and administration. I do not generalize from this, for there are indeed in many if not most congregations laypersons qualified to detect deviations from the apostolic faith. But I doubt that any of them would question the necessity for a trained and authorized Ministry.

The Roman Catholic Position as Defined at Vatican II

To conclude this survey with a look at the current situation in the Roman Catholic Church, we must refer to the papers of John Hotchkin, Kilian McDonnell, and George Tavard.

In his study on Vatican II's statements on the Christian Priesthood, John Hotchkin notes that the council aimed at extending the unfinished work of Vatican I which had been interrupted by war. A fuller presentation of the role and office of the episcopacy was needed. The presentation was needed in more than hierarchical or bureaucratic or "totem pole" terms.

Hotchkin comments that the results "would not seem to offer a very promising frame of reference for a broad and searching ecumenical dialogue on the ministry" (page 191). He cites excerpts from them which to Lutherans would seem hard-line, such as the following: ". . . the Sacred Council teaches that bishops by divine institution have succeeded to the place of the Apostles, as shepherds of the Church, and he who hears them, hears Christ, and he who rejects them, rejects Christ and Him who sent Christ. . . . For from the tradition . . . it is clear that by means of the imposition of hands and the words of consecration, the grace of the Holy Spirit is so conferred, and the sacred character so impressed that bishops in an eminent and visible way sustain the roles of Christ Himself as Teacher, Shepherd and High Priest, and that they act in His Person. . . . Priest-presbyters, the council affirms, 'do not possess the highest degree of the priesthood . . . and are dependent on the bishops in the exercise of their power'" (pages 191–192).

Differing Interpretations

All of this is by way of answer to our original question. Who may administer the sacrament? Is the sacrament valid if it is administered by someone not so permitted? In other words, is the validity of the Eucharist so essentially related to an episcopally ordained ministry that churches which do not require episcopal ordination cannot be said to have a valid ministry and a valid Eucharist? The answer would be yes for many Roman Catholic commentators on the council, Hotchkin says. However, he cites other commentators who, because of the implications of other council affirmations, believe that the work of Vatican II is also unfinished and that there is need for further work to be done on the subject. The tradition is not all that consistent and clear. ". . . The sentences formulating the collegiality of bishops are perfectly coherent and show a definite criterion, those relating to the presbyterial college suffer from a certain ambiguity, with some positive elements and other apparently contradictory ones" (Quoted from Tomas Garcia Barbena, page 197). We are contrasting bishops and priests here. We are not just talking about whether priests alone have the authority to administer a valid sacrament. We are asking whether priests who are not bishops have any authority apart from the authority conveyed to them by the bishops who have the succession vested in them.

The Common Role of Bishops and Priests

Vatican I had declared: "If anyone says that bishops are not superior to priests; or that they do not have the power to confirm and ordain, or that they have it in common with priests . . . let him be condemned." But in 1946 Rome extended the administration of confirmation to presbyters. With respect to ordination, Hotchkin styles Vatican II's formulation as "still more reserved." It speaks of bishops as the "original" ministers of ordination and "simply referred to as 'dispensers of sacred orders' with no further emphasis or elaboration on the point" (page 200).

It is sufficient, Hotchkin states, to focus only on the passages which speak of the *differences* between priest-bishops and priest-presbyters; one must also consider the council's statements on the *unity* of the two. For example: "Priests, prudent cooperators with the episcopal order, its aid and instrument, called to serve the people of God, constitute one priesthood with their bishop although bound by a diversity of duties" (page 197). The council called them "mirror images."

The Complexity of Reinterpretation

For a Protestant, it is most revealing to learn of the number of draft statements prepared for Vatican II and the reasons for changes made in them when adopting the final declarations. The problem was obvious. For centuries it had been stated that "There is no salvation outside of the Church," and this was popularly understood by the laity (and no doubt some clergy) to mean the *Roman Catholic* Church. A special situation existed with respect to the Eastern Orthodox church; no doubt it was included in some modified way. But Protestants were out! In more recent times the teaching was much less harsh: there were "separated brethren" in other churches who because their personal faith was in accord with Roman Catholic teachings of the apostolic faith were indeed Christians, but that was not to say that the churches which had baptized and nurtured them in their faith were true churches. This concession did not please all Roman Catholics. Not too many years prior to Vatican II, a priest in Boston was expelled from the church because he insisted on continuing to teach that no one could be saved outside of the Roman Catholic Church.

The delicate problem, then, was one of how to reinterpret any doctrine of the church without reversing it and thereby undermining the authority of earlier councils and popes. As we said in the second chapter, one way to do this is to point out that earlier statements spoke to specific situations, and that the circumstances have since changed—thus requiring a new interpretation. Another is to discern wider implications or underdeveloped nuances in traditional doctrines. Indeed, at Vatican II as at earlier councils, some matters were phrased deliberately in an ambiguous way, not to avoid the issue or to mislead, but to indicate that there was not a consensus so that time must be allowed for further deliberation.

A Specific Example

In the first two paragraphs of his study paper, Kilian McDonnell illustrates the reinterpretation process as it took place at the Second Vatican Council (pages 307–309). He notes that neither of the first two drafts of the *Constitution on the Church* apply the term *church* to Protestant denominations; in fact, the first preliminary draft included the clause ". . . that is why rightly only the Catholic Church is called (the) Church" (omitted in the final draft). The final text, however, included the sentence (with reference to Protestants): "They also recognize and receive other sacraments within their own churches or ecclesial communities" (Chapter 1, Article 15). One must read the succeeding paragraphs in McDonnell's paper to grasp the implications of such a sentence. The Constitution's clear intent is to affirm that the *fullness* of the manifestation of the Church is determined by the manner and extent to which the signs are evident. Thus, "For it is through Christ's Catholic Church alone, which is the all-embracing means of salvation, that the fullness of the means of salvation can be obtained" (*Decree on Ecumenism,* Article 3).

The True Church

The *Constitution* written by Vatican II, declares: "This church (the true church of Christ). . . . subsists in the Catholic Church, which is governed by the successor of Peter and by the bishops in union with that successor, although many elements of sanctification and truth can be found outside of her visible structure" (Chapter 1, Article 8, parentheses added). McDonnell comments that the word subsists was carefully chosen for its ambiguity (page 311). The complexity of language is evident. Not all Roman Catholic theologians would agree with this.

This inside account of how the Council wrestled with the subtleties of language may arouse in Protestants more impatience than understanding. Here, as at a later point in the dialogue, I thought I discerned a contradiction of terms, as in the phrase "slightly pregnant." Surely a church is in the Body of Christ or it isn't! But this is to ignore the soul-searching struggle which Vatican II undertook with integrity toward its past, while seeking guidance from the Spirit for faithful witness in the present and future.

Implications for the Ministry

A more complicated problem arises here. It is the question of whether Holy Communion can be valid in churches which do not accept other actions as sacraments, that is, confirmation, penance, ordination, marriage. As Vatican II discussed whether other churches are churches, it had to discuss this. McDonnell notes that "According to the *Decree,* (of Vatican

II on relations to other churches) the communion is not a full expression of the sacramental reality of Christ in the sacrament of orders . . . . 'The ecclesial Communities separated from us . . . lack that fullness of unity which should flow from baptism, and we believe that especially because of the lack of the sacrament of order (ordination) they have not preserved the genuine and total reality of the eucharistic mystery.' Given the fact that in the Roman church the only way to authenticate ministry is by ritual validation, in which the role of a bishop is essential, the council could not have declared otherwise and Pope Paul could not have considered any other position . . . the validity of the sacrament depends upon the validity of the ministerial office" (pages 321–322, parentheses added).

Other Possible Interpretations

We see the same points coming up again and again. Is the sacrament valid if it is not administered by a minister who is duly ordained? Is the ordination considered a sacrament? Is the ordination by a bishop who is properly in succession? Does all of this exclude a sacrament administered in a church which is not in full unity with the Bishop of Rome? Does this exclude the sacrament administered in emergency situations? Are not all situations emergency situations, considering the disunity? But . . . .

I hope you have sensed that the participants were not going round and round in argument as they kept reconsidering these issues. They were struggling again and again to satisfy these genuine concerns, while trying to recognize the sincerity in the struggles of the past when the same questions were agonizingly discussed.

McDonnell restates the reservations: "One would not want to quarrel with the principle that an authentic or valid eucharist depends on an authentic or valid ministry. I know of no Protestant theologian who would reject this as a principle. But one could argue that there is more than one avenue of access to the mystery of Christ and to the ministerial realities to which that mystery gives expression. Orders conferred by a bishop, which is one avenue of access, is not the only one. Elsewhere I have argued that one cannot tie valid ministry or valid eucharist to the possession of episcopal orders in the communion . . . there are other styles of ministry possible which are validated ecclesiologically (where there is a true though incomplete manifestation of the church, there one has a true ministry) or validated charismatically (if the Corinthian church order was authentic and valid in the New Testament times, could it not be authentic and valid today?)" (page 322).

A similar conclusion is found in the brief paper by George Tavard. He lists the several types of traditional Roman Catholic objections to a recognition of a Protestant Ministry. He concludes by stating: "Taking account of the fact that there is some evidence that both the early centuries and the Middle Ages did entertain a concept of presbyterial succession, I would be prepared to go further, and to admit that episcopal succession is not absolutely required for valid ordination . . . This conclusion is tied to a theology of the priesthood which sees no difference between priests and bishops as far as orders go, the difference lying in the order of jurisdiction, authority, and mission" (page 305). Remember that while these are responsible Roman Catholic theologians speaking, they voice only their own opinions.

The Underlying Issue

This last quotation hints at a long-standing debate which we have not yet mentioned: Is succession the only way, or is it just the best way of preserving an authentic Ministry and maintaining the unity of the church. It is an agonizing question, for if a true Christian church requires ordination by bishops in unbroken succession back to the apostles, then few Protestant churches can qualify.

We could say, just have the Roman Catholic bishops reordain all Protestant clergy and that would validate any ministry for those who considered the validity in doubt, and it wouldn't invalidate anything. But obviously the solution is not that easy. We would say, "Hold it. We can't resolve the whole issue by the touch of a hand." The Roman Catholic participants recognized that.

Nor do we attempt to decide whether recognition by the Roman Catholic Church would be constitutive of validity or merely confirmatory of existing ordination.

The Element of Faith

Speaking personally as one who is not a recognized theologian, it seems to me to boil down to the question of trust.

Perhaps I can best illustrate this by an anecdote. My uncle, for whom farming was one of many skills, was a fundamentalist who studied the Bible as his chief avocation. Unlike some of this category, he had a great sense of humor. One day while we were pitching hay he told me about a man who went to his pastor in great perplexity. "Pastor, I believe that God inspired every word in the Scriptures and so each one must be true. But I was reading the other day about a time when the lion and the lamb will be lying down together. It's in the Bible so it must be true, but I know something about animals. When it happens I'll bet you anything that the lamb will be *inside* the lion!"

I had related this story in a discussion in India where churches were trying to find a compromise . . . so they could live together in unity. The solution there was that in a united church it would not be necessary to reordain the clergy coming from churches which did not consecrate them in apostolic succession, but that all those to be ordained in the future would receive episcopal orders from Angelican bishops entering the Church of South India. In other words, the validity of non-episcopal ordination would be recognized initially, but would thereafter cease to exist; the lamb would be inside the lion. An Episcopal participant exclaimed, "That's a typical bigoted Lutheran position!"

How Does One Discern the Leading of the Spirit?

But the issue is no joke for either Lutherans or Roman Catholics. For Lutherans, authentic apostolic faith is the essential thing; and while juridical ordination in apostolic succession may well bear testimony to that authenticity, it does not automatically guarantee it. As I understand the Roman Catholic position, it places equal emphasis upon the apostolic faith as indispensible; but tends to add to this a greater trust that the episcopal office functioning under the guidance of the Holy Spirit has preserved and will protect this same faith. Lutherans, licking their wounds from the past, profess no lack of faith in the Holy Spirit but insist that the touchstones must be gospel, to which the episcopal office may be a tremendously beneficial and unifying witness—which it has not always been in the past. Add to this tension the problem that not all Protestant churches think the way Lutheran churches do.

At the San Francisco meeting of the dialogues, a Catholic participant said to me, "Paul, I'm fully persuaded that the

Lutheran Ministry is valid for it has a precedent in the early church and that to maintain our integrity, Catholics must say so. But I shudder to think what this will mean with respect to our relationships with the Orthodox and Anglican churches!" The Anglican and Orthodox churches are very anxious too that the Ministry be properly ordered with proper succession. If the Roman Catholic Church is earnest in its desire to have unity with Lutherans, it must be just as earnest in its desire to have unity with other churches.

The basic question is, what doctrine of the Ministry does each church hold and how can we find agreement in those doctrines. Sadly but honestly the report answers that: "The dialogue group stated: Neither Catholic nor Lutheran participants came to this dialogue with a complete doctrine of this Ministry and we have not formulated one in our discussions." As long as this question remains unanswered, complete agreement has not been reached. Have we brought you this far only to say it was all futile? It would be futile if we did not see an ongoing earnest desire to work out the problems.

Related Considerations

At the first meeting between Catholic bishops and Lutheran presidents in Washington, DC in 1975, it was evident that the bishops found the dialogue on the Ministry to be less than clear in its findings. One bishop asked whether, given that nonepiscopal ordination did happen at some time as an isolated incident, such a procedure can be acceptable as a norm. He was told by Catholic theologians present that what was done once could be done again if there were sufficient reasons for doing so, and that presbyterial succession in orders, a possibility maintained by St. Jerome, has always been an open question in the Catholic Church and was left as such at the Second Vatican Council. The minutes of this meeting record an agreement that while isolated instances should not be regarded as norms, New Testament varieties in practice cannot be ignored, and that what has happened at one time in the history of the church could possibly happen again.

At that same meeting, a Catholic theologian remarked that Roman Catholics have not said that Lutherans are unsaved if they do not accept dogmas about Mary or papal primacy. The Lutherans are not even considered indifferent to truth for not accepting those dogmas.

Another commented that he had not previously taken into account the fact that while he himself felt bound by such decisions as those made at the Council of Trent (against Lutheran teachings), he now realized that there had been prior to Trent elements in the Catholic tradition to which the Lutheran reformers accurately appealed. I related the instance of a Lutheran church in Yugoslavia which when that area had been part of the Austro-Hungarian empire, had had all of its pastors ejected for a period of about fifty years. During that time, laymen preached and administered the sacraments and the church maintained and increased its strength. I asked whether Roman Catholics would say that none of the promises of Christ were fulfilled during the celebrations of Holy Communion because no valid ministers presided? One theologian responded that on the basis of present Roman Catholic teaching, he could neither affirm nor deny it.

Apparently there is room for further discussion. I regard it as hopeful that the common statement in which all Catholic participants joined has not been officially rejected in the nine years since it first appeared.

Is All This Really Crucial?

This chapter is long. Is the subject really that important? No doubt most, if not all, Lutheran pastors would endorse my comment that when serving a parish, I couldn't have cared less whether or not my ordination was regarded as valid by Roman Catholics! But if the question of the Ministry is *the* major obstacle to Christian unity, it cannot be lightly dismissed. Don't get your hopes up, for no final answers are in view. Don't despair, either, but join me in regarding these studies and dialogues as part of the workings of the Holy Spirit among us. As pilgrims, we've made a lot of progress. Though I may not live to see the daylight, I rejoice that I begin to see glimmerings of the dawn.

Dilemmas for discussion:

1. Must the sacrament be administered only by a minister or may it be administered by anyone?
2. Must the minister be ordained or may the minister be anyone who is appointed?
3. Must the ordination be by a bishop or may it be by anyone acting on vote of a congregation or synod?

4. Must the bishop be appointed in succession from the apostles or may the bishop be anyone chosen by vote?

DISCUSSION

Suggestions for a Discussion of the Ministry

- The group could discuss the following case study:

  In the days when North America was being settled by Europeans, many Roman Catholics and Lutherans lived in villages not served by a priest or pastor. In some cases Lutherans gathered and elected a pastor and ordained him. The Catholics, however, used only priests ordained by bishops who were appointed by apostolic succession.
  Do you think the Lutherans should have waited to get a minister ordained by a bishop?
  Do you think neither Lutherans nor Catholics should have communed without a priest or pastor present to preside?

- The group could suppose that a situation developed in which many people at a private summer camp were administering Communion "just to try it out" whether they believed or not, and, using any words whether the words referred to Christ or not. Suppose that a nearby church whose people had been going to the camp would issue a statement saying that Communion isn't really being administered if it isn't under certain conditions. What should those conditions be?
  The point of this is to discuss how much order is necessary for Communion, and how much authority the church should take in maintaining order.

Suppose that the conditions your church decides upon are different from those others decide upon. What would you do if you wanted to commune together?

The group could also suppose that Christians of various churches are thrown together in a prison camp which has neither priest nor pastor. Should they commune, and if so, how would they decide on the words to be used and the order?

CHAPTER 5

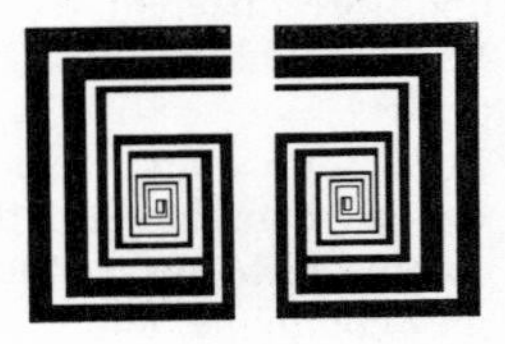

Papal Primacy and the Universal Church

More than a few people were startled when picking up their newspapers on March 4, 1974. The *New York Times* and other prominent papers had printed front-page stories with headlines such as "Catholics and Lutherans Reach Accord on the Papacy." The *Christian Science Monitor* ran a special feature on the matter. Before too long I received the translation of a Latin American journal article entitled "Lutherans Accept Papal Authority"!

Predictably, some Lutherans reacted sharply to these reports. Letters written to *The Lutheran* shortly thereafter contained such expressions as "I am outraged . . ."; "I was abhorred by the article . . ."; "How tragic . . ."; and so on. Generally, however, the mood was one of bewilderment. Why, we were asked, waste the time to discuss such a subject at all? Have Luther's protests been aborted? What about his "Here I stand"? What about the deviations from the gospel which he observed in the papal-dominated Roman Catholic Church of his day? So what if some Roman Catholics now have problems with the dogma on the papacy, "It's their headache; let them find their own aspirin," we were told.

Such talk is nonsense. We can allow for misgivings which were aroused by exaggerations in the press, and we can respect a genuine concern that the principles of the Reformation not be forgotten; but outright disdain for efforts toward unity reflects arrogance rather than Christian humility and love. It's our problem too. The church is one Body, the members of which must function in behalf of the mission of that Body as a whole. This mission is obstructed by a contentiousness which is seen by the world-at-large as a scandal. The sectarianism belies our claims of Christian faith and forfeits the respect of those on the outside.

Again, we admit, the headlines were misleading. No, Lutherans did not and do not accept papal primacy. The common statement issued by the two groups of theologians was cautiously worded, and hedged with many stipulations. Nevertheless, it does provide an updated context from which a fresh approach can be made.

Nontheological Dimensions

I have assessed the question regarding a "valid ministry" as being perhaps the most critical in relation to bridging the separation between Lutherans and Roman Catholics. The question about the pope comes in the same colors. If the doctrine of a valid ministry is in question, that focuses on the pope because the pope is the apex of the Ministry in the Roman Catholic Church. Pope Paul VI himself stated that "The pope—as we all know—is undoubtedly the gravest obstacle in the path of ecumenism."

The problems are not only theological and historical but also highly emotional. Since Reformation times, members on each side have been conditioned to regard each other with suspicion and distrust. Many Lutherans know that Article IV of the *Smalcald Articles* in the Lutheran Confession tears the pope apart, calling him the "very Anti-Christ," and the Appendix to these articles elaborates on this in detail.

Such emotional prejudices are not easily erased. Few are aware that the arguments in support of this article are directed not so much against the office itself as against the abuse of the office and unbiblical claims made for the office. The claims are spelled out in Part I of the Appendix.

I have good reasons to know this! In July of 1960, during a series of theological discussions between the National Lutheran Council and the Lutheran Church—Missouri Synod in Chicago which led to the formation of the Lutheran Council in the U.S.A., I raised this very issue. I noted that at a convention in the 50s, the LCMS had reaffirmed its "Brief Statement" of 1931 as binding upon all of its pastors and teachers, including the affirmation that the pope is the Antichrist. My comment was that since Article VII of *The Augsburg Confes-*

sion states that for the unity of the church it is enough to agree upon the doctrine of the gospel and the administration of the sacraments, one would have to conclude that the teaching about the pope as the Antichrist was a part of the doctrine of the gospel; that I for one accepted neither the teaching nor its place in a binding category, despite the statement in the Lutheran Confessions. At that moment I suffered a major heart attack (the timing of which may raise some LCMS eyebrows!). While waiting to be taken to the hospital in the nick of time, I dimly heard the explanation given that today this article is construed as meaning that insofar as the pope interposes himself adversely between the church and the gospel, he is a *type* of the Antichrist. Now they tell us!

Let me add parenthetically that this emotional factor works both ways. When our film *Martin Luther* was released in the 50s, a friend of mine was standing in line at a downtown theater in Philadelphia. Above his head was a poster depicting Luther at the Diet of Worms, his mouth wide open as he declared "Here I stand," words which Lutherans cherish. A bystander with a heavy Irish brogue looked at it and said to her friend, "Look at him; you can see the very sin and evil staring right out of his face!" Happily, we can discuss this issue today in a more dispassionate mood, perhaps more because of the widespread television coverage given to recent popes as the great Christian leaders they are than because of our effrots to set the record straight. However, it is noteworthy that Lutheran leaders the world over as well as the executive committee of the Lutheran World Federation sent cordial greetings to Pope John Paul I, mourned his death, and assured Pope John Paul II of their prayers "that your ministry will be a blessing to all Christians."

The Issue Defined

Immediately we must point out that papal *primacy* is different from papal *infallibility.* Infallibility has to do with the truth in what the pope teaches. Primacy has to do with being the leader of the church.

The common statement on papal primacy published in 1974 attempts to set the record straight. Issues and remaining disagreements are openly discussed; nothing is swept under the rug. One must keep in mind that it deals with papal *primacy,* that is to say, the role of the papal office in symbolizing, furthering, and guarding the unity of the church and possessing the God-given final authority in decision making. That means the same as the words of the motto on President Truman's desk, "The buck stops here." This is different from papal infallibility in his teaching role about doctrine, which may be far more difficult to resolve and is considered separately in the following chapter.

Remember that when discussing the ministry, it was agreed that the general ministry of proclaiming the gospel is the vocation of the whole people of God, but the apostolic church was led to establish a special Ministry of word and sacrament to unify and order the church for its mission in and to the world. (Again, the capital "M" distinguishes, but does not elevate the clergy.) The discussion now focuses upon the question: If the Ministry is to unify the church, how can it bring together separated churches? The question is examined from its historical aspects, beginning with the biblical evidence, its theological basis and implications, and with regard to the practical consequences arising from the conclusions drawn from the results of these historical and theological investigations.

Peter and the Petrine Function

The group commissioned a panel of New Testament scholars to examine the role of Peter to ascertain whether or not there is a biblical foundation for calling the pope Peter's successor. (These findings, published in a paperback entitled *Peter in the New Testament,* are unique, highly regarded, and widely quoted; they have been translated into several languages.) The results are somewhat mixed. Peter certainly was the most prominent leader among the Twelve. True, the Scriptures tell how he was rebuked by Christ (who even called him "Satan" shortly after he called him a "Rock"); and true, they tell how Peter later denied Christ. Yet, true also, Peter is reported as the one instructed to strengthen the faith of his brethren and to feed and tend Christ's sheep. But there is no indication in the New Testament that he was to have a successor or that his role was the initiation of a perpetual *office.*

The common statement notes that " . . . we have no trustworthy evidence that Peter ever served as the supervisor or bishop of the local church in Rome" (page 14). Yet the growth and spread of the church was accompanied by quarrels and dissentions. Paul and other writers of the New Testament epistles refer to many disputes and Paul claimed authority from Christ in seeking to resolve some of them. In later developments, Peter was gradually given the image of a pastor caring for the universal church (documented in the study papers of McCue and Piepkorn, pages 43–97).

From this arose the concept of a Petrine Function, a term used to describe a particular form of Ministry exercised by a person, office-holder, or local church with reference to the church as a whole (page 11).

Insofar as the New Testament evidence is concerned, the scholars conclude that "an investigation of the historical career does not necessarily settle the question of Peter's importance for the subsequent church." The foundations for the *model* of the papacy as it ultimately developed in the Western church cannot be discerned in the New Testament itself.

McCue and Piepkorn also recount the early years of the church. The appearance of heresies and widespread deviations in practice made some kind of church order imperative. Gradually over a 200-year period, local Western churches tended to turn to Rome for support in settling problems. This was partly because according to tradition the church in Rome was taught personally by Peter and Paul (who were executed there) and thus came to be regarded as a center of orthodoxy (fidelity to apostolic teaching). Another factor undoubtedly was the place of Rome as the capital of the empire and a center of communications. This development took place in what is named the Patristic Era.

Developments in the Early Centuries

As scholars move through the Patristic Era and into the subsequent centuries they find an uneven, but noticeable trend to claim supreme ecclesiastical authority for the papacy. Theological opinions on the subject varied, but popes themselves steadily assumed wider power.

Most Protestants will be astonished at the readiness with which Catholic historians concede the flaws in the record: the quarrels and contentiousness; the maneuvering for power; the abuses of authority; the fact that some popes were declared heretics by their successors; and the scandal during one period when rival popes claimed the office in Italy and France simultaneously, each presumptor denouncing the other.

Papal claims grew to the extravagant declaration of

Boniface VIII (1294–1303) that the Bishop of Rome had authority over secular rulers. Boniface also went so far as to say that it is necessary to salvation for everyone to be subject to the Roman pontiff.

The Other Side of the Picture

But there are two sides to the development; it must be viewed in perspective. Over the centuries there were very many popes whose spiritual insights and dynamic leadership not only served to protect and preserve the apostolic faith, but also provided a bulwark against political authorities who repeatedly tried to take control of the church. Lutheran leaders have had to wrestle with this problem, and still do in some countries. As the Lutheran participants put it in their *Reflections*, "Lutheranism . . . suffered from subservience to state power. Its own ecclesiastical authorities have not always fostered Christian liberty and faithfulness to the gospel. It too reacted defensively to intellectual and cultural movements. Worst of all, in many places it came close to losing the vision of the unity of God's people. In view of this record, Lutherans have no ground for self-righteousness" (page 26). The issue today is not one of measuring perfection in leadership, past or present, but rather of seeking Spirit-led consensus on the structures which best serve the gospel and foster the unity of the church in our time.

Divine Right Versus Human Right

In the debates which raged during the Reformation period, sharp distinctions were made between those practices in the church which were based on divine right (or institution) and human (or ecclesial) right. The former is mandatory; the latter can be changed. The Roman Catholic Church had traditionally declared papal supremacy to be divinely instituted and thus binding. Lutherans have countered that the office was developed by human decisions and thus is optional according to circumstances. With his signing of the *Smalcald Articles*, Melanchthon wrote: "However, concerning the pope I hold that, if he would allow the Gospel, we, too, may concede to him that superiority over the bishops which he possesses by human right, making this concession for the sake of peace and general unity among the Christians who are now under him and who may be in the future'' (*The Book of Concord*, pages 316–317).

The common statement records: ''While we have concluded that traditional sharp distinctions between divine and human institution are no longer useful, Catholics continue to emphasize that papal primacy is an institution in accordance with God's will. For Lutherans this is a secondary question. The one thing necessary, they insist, is that papal primacy serve the gospel and that its exercise of power not subvert Christian freedom'' (page 22). The Catholic participants expand upon this point in their *Reflections*: ''The common statement, however, does not fully reflect everything that we believe concerning the papacy. The acceptance of the papal office is for us imperative because we believe that it is willed by God for his church. The mission entrusted to the church by Christ is served by the papacy. In it God has given us a sign of unity and an instrument for Christian life and mission. Therefore we affirm the traditional Roman Catholic position that the papacy is, in a true sense, 'divinely instituted' '' (page 34).

The difference between the Lutheran and Catholic views is coming clear here. The Lutheran Confessions tend to equate ''divine right'' with a clear command found in the Scriptures, whereas human rights are defined as *useful* institutions and practices which the word of God explicitly neither commands nor forbids. In their *Reflections,* the Catholic participants approach the subject in a different context. They seem to see no clear dividing line between where the New Testament leaves off and the apostolic work continues: ''We believe that the New Testament is given to us not as a finished body of doctrine but as an expression of the developing faith and institutionalization of the church in the first century.''

''In many respects, the New Testament and the doctrines it contains are complemented by subsequent developments in the faith and life of the church. . . .''

As Roman Catholics we are convinced that the papal and episcopal form of Ministry, as it concretely evolved, is a divinely-willed sequel to the functions exercised respectively by Peter and the other apostles according to various NT traditions'' (pages 34–35).

God's Will Versus Human Understanding

The problem lies in the difficulty of separating the will of God from the human instruments through which that will must operate. The Acts of the Apostles quotes decisions as being certified by the words "It has seemed good to the Holy Spirit and to us. . . ." The authority of these chosen companions of Christ was accepted by all. Without the guidance of the Holy Spirit throughout its history, the church has no claim to be other than a creation of human beings. But how is the authenticity of the Spirit's guidance to be verified? When Paul said that women should keep quiet in the church (1 Corinthians 14:34), was he relaying an instruction from the Spirit binding for all time (since he said he spoke with the Lord's authority), or was he counseling a time-bound regulation influenced by the social and cultural circumstances of his time? If one discerns God's will in the development of the papacy in the Western church, does this mean that the Holy Spirit's guidance was lacking in the different church orders which developed in the Eastern Orthodox churches? Was Luther guided by the Holy Spirit when he called for reforms in the Roman Catholic Church of his day or was only the Council of Trent, which condemned his teachings, guided by that same Spirit? The history of the church is filled with bitter controversies over matters of faith and order, each side claiming divine sanction. Surely it is necessary to identify those central, indispensible teachings of the apostolic faith so closely tied to the gospel that without them what remains cannot be called Christian at all. However, the difficulty of weighing the human factor in explicating God's will would indeed seem to make the use of the terms *divine* and *human* not very useful. Other ways must be found.

The Contemporary Situation

Does all this leave us at a stalemate? We hope not! The common statement notes (1) that the Catholic members see the institution of the papacy as developing from New Testament roots under the guidance of the Spirit and as God's gracious gift to his people, and that (2) the Lutheran members, while recognizing many positive papal contributions to the life of the church (despite past defects) still cannot accept the pope as the divinely willed supreme earthly head of the *universal* church. Both sides agree that just as the forms of the papacy have been adapted to changing historical settings in the past, they may be modified to meet the needs of the church in the future (page 19, paraphrased).

Three principles are stated:

Legitimate Diversity. Since the ultimate authority is God revealed in Christ, and since all members share in the guidance and judgment of the Spirit, they should recognize that the Spirit's guidance may give rise to diverse forms in piety, liturgy, theology, custom, or law. While the forms may be different, they should never foster divisiveness.

Collegiality. Since no one person or administrative staff, however dedicated, can grasp all the local situations in a worldwide church, and because a local church may be stifled in the way it deals with a local situation if authority is excessively centralized, all parts of the church should share in the concern and responsibilities of leadership.

Subsidiarity. Every section of the church should exercise the gifts it has received from the Spirit while remaining mindful of its heritage. What properly can be decided and done in smaller units of ecclesial life ought not to be referred to church leaders who have wider responsibilities. Wholesome diversity should be encouraged, and minority viewpoints protected within the unity of faith.

The Watershed of Vatican II

The historic declarations of the Second Vatican Council (1962–1965) provide the basis for healing the wounds of the sixteenth century. How is this possible given the Catholic tradition that dogmas are irreversible? The answer merits a quotation of some length. The *Reflections* of the Catholic participants state (pages 35–36):

> "The teaching of this council (Vatican I [1870]) should be understood according to the context of the times in which it was formulated and the intention of the council fathers. To this end we may now call attention to some principles recently articulated by the Congregation for the Doctrine of the Faith with regard to the historical conditioning of Dogmatic formulations. In a declaration dated June 24, 1973, the following four factors are set forth:
>
> **a.** The meaning of the pronouncements of faith depends partly upon the expressive power of the language used at a certain point in time and in particular circumstances.

b. Sometimes a dogmatic truth is first expressed incompletely, but not falsely, and later more fully and perfectly in a broader context of faith and human knowledge.
c. When the church makes new pronouncements, it not only confirms what is in some way contained in scripture or previous expressions of tradition; usually it also has the intention of solving specific questions or removing specific errors.
d. Sometimes the truths the church intends to teach through its dogmatic formulations may be enunciated in terms that bear traces of the changeable conceptions of a given epoch.

"In confronting the specific problems and errors of its time, Vatican Council I sensed that a concentration on the papacy was crucially important, in order to safeguard the church's evangelical freedom from political pressures and its universality in an age of divisive national particularism. Yet the council tended to accent the juridical aspects of the papacy more than the church needs would require in the broader context of our times. It has become apparent that papal Ministry, as a spiritual and evangelical task, can and needs to find a 'fuller and more perfect expression' than was possible at Vatican Council I. Vatican Council II has already begun this process. . . .

"A general directive was given by Christ to his disciples: 'Earthly kings lord it over their people . . . yet it cannot be that way with you' (Luke 22: 25–26). In keeping with this directive, the doctrine concerning the papacy must be understood in ways that recognize the church's total subordination to Christ and the gospel and its obligation to respect the rights of all individuals, groups, and offices both within the church and beyond its limits. Monarchical absolutism in the church would violate the command of Christ" (parentheses and brackets added).

The Lutheran reaction to this kind of interpretation was that if such views should prevail, the matter of "papal primacy will no longer be open to so many traditional Lutheran objections." Many objections would be satisfied. *Many,* but, unfortunately, not all.

Esse Versus *Bene Esse*

A question remains: Is the papacy of the *esse* or the *bene esse* of the church? Is it of the essence, or is it just a good practice? The Roman Catholic tradition as defined at Vatican I stresses its essence, while many Lutherans (but not all) might accept it as good practice under certain conditions. If Lutherans were to accept the official Roman Catholic position, they would be virtually conceding that their churches have not been and are not true Christian churches. On the other hand, if they take the biblical witness seriously that Christ wills his followers to be one, they must admit that their own structures do not provide a good model for the church as a whole. In considering options, might a reinterpreted papal primacy provide an effective one?

In their *Reflections* (page 21), the Lutheran participants note that "Lutherans increasingly recognize the need for a Ministry serving the unity of the church universal. They acknowledge that, for the exercise of this Ministry, institutions which are rooted in history should be seriously considered. The church should use the signs of unity it has received, for new ones cannot be invented at will. Thus the Reformers wished to continue the historic structures of the church." The statement goes on to affirm that the papacy has often served a beneficial role in the past, that God may lead it to do so in the future, and to suggest that such a role in relation to Lutherans might be more pastoral than juridical. "*The one thing necessary, from the Lutheran point of view, is that papal primacy be so structured and interpreted that it clearly serve the gospel and the unity of the church of Christ, and that its exercise of power not subvert Christian freedom*" (page 21, emphasis added). This, in short, would describe a *bene esse* role.

The Papacy in the Hierarchy of Truths

Is there a serious roadblock to convergence of views on this point? Many Roman Catholics think not. The Bull of Boniface VIII had said that every human who is not subject to the Roman pontiff is unsaved. Tavard in his study of the Bull concluded that it does not meet the Vatican I criteria for an infallible statement. It can be questioned. Papal primacy is not accepted by the Eastern Orthodox churches, which Roman Catholics acknowledge to be authentic churches. To affirm that the papacy developed in the Western church under the guidance of the Holy Spirit is not to restrict God's will as to other developments. The questions raised by Catholic participant Patrick Burns are directed to this issue: "All admit that God's will in these areas is always mediated by human arrangements which concretize . . . in the area of divine law, does the will of God for a structured sacramental church *in* history necessarily preclude real change at a later period of history and in a different cultural context?" (page 171).

The question must be asked: Is papal primacy so central to the gospel or so high in the hierarchy of truths that its rejection ends all possibilities for fellowship? The participants in this discussion seem to suggest that it is not. As Joseph Baker asked about the dogmas on Mary and papal infallibility: ". . . Is it possible for the Catholic Church to affirm that positive acceptance of the dogmas proclaimed during the period of mutual schism is not an absolute requirement for unity?" and ". . . can we expect them (Lutherans) to affirm that these doctrines are not contrary to revelation?" (page 220, parentheses added). Or as the Catholic participants put it in their *Reflections*: "Could not the pope in our time become in some real way pastor and teacher of all the faithful, even those who cannot accept all the claims connected with his office?" (pages 37–38). In other words, how much organizational and theological diversity is possible without rupturing the unity we profess to have in one Lord and his gospel?

Conclusions of the Common Statement

After reflecting upon the many facets of the issue, the participants listed the following agreements as significant:

"—Christ wills for his church a unity which is not only spiritual, but must be manifest in the world.
—Promotion of this unity is incumbent on all believers, especially those who are engaged in the Ministry of word and sacrament.
—The greater the responsibility of a ministerial office, the greater the responsibility to seek the unity of all Christians.
—A special responsibility for this may be entrusted to one individual Minister, under the Gospel.
—Such a responsibility for the universal church cannot be ruled out on the basis of the biblical evidence.

—The bishop of Rome, whom Roman Catholics regard as entrusted by the will of Christ with this responsibility, and who has exercised his Ministry in forms that have changed significantly over the centuries, can in the future function in ways which are better adapted to meet both the universal and regional needs of the church in the complex environment of modern times'' (page 22).

It will be noted that these statements include both agreements and cautiously worded hopes. The authors admit that they haven't explored to what extent the existing forms of the papal office are open to change in the future. The important achievement is the clearing of a way for the churches to enter into serious conversations on this subject in a spirit free of polemics, prior misunderstandings, and mistrust. The Lutheran participants stress the need for a papal primacy ''renewed in the light of the gospel.'' They add in their *Reflections:* ''Our Lutheran teaching about the church and the Ministry constrain us to believe that recognition of papal primacy is possible to the degree that a renewed papacy would in fact foster faithfulness to the gospel and truly exercises a Petrine function within the church'' (page 33). The Catholic participants affirm that the papal office does function under the gospel. Obviously, there is need to explore this affirmation further as well as the Lutheran concern that exercise of papal power ''not subvert Christian freedom.''

McDonnell quotes Vatican Council II's *Decree on Ecumenism* (Article 24) when he suggests that ''For the present, Lutherans and Catholics 'go forward without obstructing the ways of divine Providence and without prejudging the future inspiration of the Holy Spirit,' '' and adds: ''However, that future inspiration of the Holy Spirit is already now prejudged and the way toward unity is already obstructed if there is not the firm will to unity. The will to unity is defined as the readiness to translate the allegiance to one faith, one Lord, and one baptism into visible forms. The necessity of unity in faith coming to recognizable visibility is of the gospel. Finally, other than fidelity to the gospel no preconditions to the future inspirations of the Holy Spirit can be posited'' (page 193).

Practical Consequences

Although these theologians were appointed to this task by their respective churches, they could speak only for themselves. Thus it was necessary to suggest to the churches specific steps in furtherance of the possibilities opened up by these conversations.

The Lutheran churches are asked—

> "If they are prepared to affirm with us that papal primacy, *renewed* in the light of the gospel, need not be a barrier to reconciliation.
> If they are able to acknowledge not only the legitimacy of the papal Ministry in the service of the Roman Catholic communion but even the possibility and the desirability of the papal Ministry, *renewed under the gospel and committed to Christian freedom,* in a larger communion which would include the Lutheran churches.
> If they are willing to open discussion regarding the concrete implications of *such a primacy* to them" (emphases added).

The Roman Catholic Church is asked—

> "If in the light of our findings, it should not give high priority in its ecumenical concerns to the problem of reconciliation with the Lutheran churches.
> If it is willing to open discussions on possible structures for reconciliation which would protect the legitimate traditions of the Lutheran communities and respect their spiritual heritage.
> If it is prepared to envisage the possibility of reconciliation which would recognize the self-government of Lutheran churches within a communion.
> If, in the expectation of a foreseeable reconciliation, it is ready to acknowledge the Lutheran churches represented in our dialogue as sister-churches which are already entitled to some measure of ecclesiastical communion" (pages 22–23).

Such questions make it quite plain that Lutherans are far from accepting papal primacy in the presently existing situation. But the fact that the theologians had reached such a measure of agreement on basic issues that these questions could even be addressed to their churches marked a milestone—perhaps even a turning point—in their separated relationship. The closing words of the joint statement should be indelibly underscored:

"Neither church should continue to tolerate a situation in which members of one communion look upon the other as alien. Trust in the Lord who makes us one body in Christ will help us to risk ourselves on the yet undisclosed paths toward which his Spirit is guiding his church" (page 23).

Dilemmas for discussion:

1. Papal primacy compared with papal infallibility? Can one be accepted without the other?
2. Divine right compared with human right. Can two churches get together if one accepts the papal office as arranged by humans while the other accepts it as instituted by God?
3. *Esse* versus *bene esse.* Can two churches get together if one considers the papal office of the essence of the church while the other considers it a good practice, but not necessary?

DISCUSSION

Suggestions for a Discussion of Papal Primacy and Infallibility

- Have the group suppose that suddenly all the churches got together and formed one church. Also suppose that your study group itself represents leaders from the churches of the various countries which have gotten together. Would there be any way possible that the group could meet without choosing one person to lead the meeting? At the top left side of the chalkboard, list advantages of having one person lead the group. At the bottom left, list the disadvantages of having one person lead. If a person is to be chosen how would the group agree on who the leader should be, and what would be the leader's responsiblities?
- At the top right of the board, write reasons why it would be good to give a leader of the group authority to decide which teachings are true and which are not. At the bottom right, write reasons why it might not be good to give a leader authority to determine truth.
- After these two discussions are completed, at the top left of the board, write Papal Primacy and at the top right write Papal Infallibility. The purpose is to help the group recognize the difference between primacy and infallibility. As the text says, primacy has to do with organizational responsibility as in Truman's statement "The buck stops here." Infallibility has to do with doctrinal authority.

- The group could discuss which is better, decision making by a single office or by vote of a convention. Are there some matters which can be administered better by one person, and other matters better by consensus? The group could list matters which should not be decided by a popular vote. For example, the messages of the prophets would have been voted down. The group could list matters which should not be decided by a single office or person. For example, a single office might not know what was the best way of communicating the gospel in certain areas because local situations might require local experience and strategy.

CHAPTER 6

Teaching Authority and Infallibility in the Church

The dialogues on the teaching authority of the church took four years! It was a tough nut to crack, and one cannot be blamed for asking whether or not it was worth all that time and effort. Emphatically, my answer is yes it was!

Notice first of all the wording of the topic. Although *papal* infallibility was the target of the discussion, it was considered within the wider context of the teaching authority and infallibility in the *church*. This is a very complex and central issue for *all* Christians, indeed a major factor in the present divided state of the Body of Christ. Many if not most of those who have attacked the dogma of papal infallibility have not understood its purpose and limitations and actually oppose something which the Roman Catholic Church does not teach. It was officially declared only a little over a century ago, and its interpretation is still under debate within Roman Catholic circles. Protestants are surprised to find that there is no list of pronouncements officially designated as infallible, which adds to the perplexities surrounding the subject.

The Wider Implications of the Subject

Let no Christian suppose that he or she can have a field day shooting holes in the Roman Catholic claims for papal infallibility. We are all just as vulnerable on this point. We find that out when we state what we believe and then are asked why we believe it. Why do we believe it? Because it makes sense? That is saying that our powers of reason are our authority. Is our reason infallible? Why do we believe it? Because it works? That is saying that practical experience is our authority. Is our experience infallible? Why do we believe it? Because the Bible tells us so. That is saying that the Bible is our authority. As was mentioned earlier, there are those who ascribe such infallible authority to the Bible, they can be accused of substituting a "paper pope" for the pope.

We cannot assess the claims for papal infallibility without simultaneously testing our own way of verifying truth claims. The Lutheran participants learned much about the shortcomings of their own tradition in these years of sharing insights, and the experience was profitable.

The outcome was not one of complete consensus, but rather a recognition of mutual concerns and purposes. As the common statement puts it, "Papal infallibility is related to several wider questions: the authority of the gospel; the indefectibility of the Church; the infallibility of its belief and teaching; and the assurance of certainty which Christian believers have always associated with their faith" (page 12). Many devout Christians find their faith tested over and over again by these nagging questions which have no simplistic answers.

A Capsule Summary of Agreements

Before reviewing significant elements of the discussions, it may be helpful to outline briefly the consensus which did develop. It is important to be aware of this limited agreement when examining the studies of historical and doctrinal developments which led up to it.

The two groups found themselves in harmony on the following central points:

- Jesus Christ, the sole Lord of the church, discloses his will and grace through the proclamation of the gospel and the administration of the sacraments.
- The Word of God in the Scriptures is normative (that is, it provides the enduring touchstone) for all proclamation and teaching in the church.
- The apostolic tradition in which the Word of God is transmitted is normative for all other traditions which interpret it by means of creeds, liturgies, dogmas, confessions, doctrines, forms of church government and discipline, and patterns of devotion and service.

- In accordance with scriptural promises and through the continued assistance of the risen Christ effected through the Holy Spirit, the church will remain to the end of time with an *indefectibility* in which the truth of the gospel, its mission, and its life of faith will persevere.
- This indefectibility involves a Ministry of Word and Sacrament together with structures (such as, councils and synods) charged with the teaching of Christian doctrine and with the supervision and coordination of the ministry of the whole people of God, including the *mandate* for bishops or leaders to *judge doctrine* and *condemn doctrine* that is *contrary to the gospel.*
- There may be appropriately a Ministry *in the universal church* responsible to further its unity and mission.
- Such a Ministry would have the responsibility of overseeing the church's proclamation and, as needed, of *reformulating doctrine in fidelity to the Scriptures,* the *sign* of such fidelity being the *harmony between the teaching of the Ministers and its acceptance by the faithful.*
- The church in every age under the guidance of the Holy Spirit is able to find language and other forms of witness to communicate the gospel in different cultures. No human language fully expresses the richness and diversity of the gospel, and *no doctrinal definition* can *adequately* address *every* historical or cultural situation (emphases, mine).

One can easily recognize here overtones from some of the arguments which took place in the discussions on papal primacy, but there are important additions which will become clearer in the succeeding pages. Although the terms *indefectibility* and *infallibility* are not synonomous, either can be interpreted in such a way as to minimize the difference. As will be seen later on, the Lutheran concept of indefectibility and some current Catholic definitions of infallibility have much in common.

Doctrinal Authority in the Early Church

The word infallible is not used in the New Testament. The emphasis is more upon *authority.* It is stated that Christ spoke as one with "authority"; he claimed the authority to forgive sins. After his death and resurrection "all authority, in heaven and on earth" is ascribed to him. Thereafter this authority was expressed and communicated in the *gospel,* that Word of God which was passed along by those who had received it directly. Later on it was recorded by various authors to preserve in writing this oral tradition.

The gospel itself may be called infallible in the sense that it is God's promise in Christ, and as the Lutheran Confessions put it, "God does not lie." For early Christians, the authority of the gospel was twofold: the outward witness of those who had received it from Christ and the inner certification of the Holy Spirit. No one could confess Jesus as Lord apart from the work of the Holy Spirit (1 Corinthians 12:3, paraphrased).

Defining the Gospel

Earlier reference has been made to the various interpretations of this term *gospel.* I vividly recall the discussion on this subject in our talks with theologians of the Presbyterian and Reformed traditions. When the Lutherans quoted Article VII of *The Augusburg Confession* which declares that "to the true unity of the Church, it is enough to agree concerning the doctrine of the Gospel . . . ," we were pressed to state explicitly how we defined that word. We could give no clear-cut answer. The *Formula of Concord* says that "the term Gospel is not used in one and the same sense in the Holy Scriptures." On the one hand, if used in contrast to the term Law, it is the good news of God's promise of forgiveness by grace through faith in Christ's atoning life and death. But if the term is to include the entire doctrine of Christ, which he proposed in his ministry, as also did his apostles, the term includes a preaching of repentance as well as the forgiveness of sins. The common statement speaks of it as "the proclaiming of this saving action of God in the person, life, death, and resurrection of Jesus and made present in the Holy Spirit" (page 14). (My father used to tell us that John 3:16 was the most concise expression of the gospel to be found.) Later the common statement notes that "This gospel . . . is expressed in various terms, as God's righteousness, reconciliation, and forgiveness of sins. . . . One can claim, indeed, that for the first two centuries of Christianity, 'gospel' denoted 'the revelation of Christ.' " (pages 16–17).

Preserving the Deposit of Faith

The preceding paragraph should not lead one to conclude that there are serious differences between Lutherans and Roman Catholics regarding the nature or content of the gospel. Rather it provides an illustration of how words do not always mean precisely the same things to different Christian traditions. Already in the early church and in subsequent generations, bitter quarrels and schisms developed over implications of the gospel. Some criteria were necessary to recognize authentic Christian faith. Councils were convened and creeds were composed for this purpose.

Great weight was given to those churches founded by apostles, especially to the church in Rome. The common statement notes that in the year 515, the Roman pope declared that in Rome "the catholic religion has always been preserved immaculate" (page 21), a conviction that continued on into the Middle Ages. There were challenges to such claims both in the East and in the West. The orthodoxy of several popes was questioned, and the role of other apostolic churches as defenders of the true faith was emphasized. Yet gradually, in the West, "on the basis of the belief that Rome had never deviated from the truth, it came to be held that in the future Rome would be immune from error, the Roman church or the Roman bishop can not err" (page 22).

The Arrival of Infallibility Language

Although the term *infallible* had been used earlier regarding God's truth, the revelation, and normative teachings of the universal church, it was not until the thirteen and fourteenth centuries that it came to be applied expressly to the formal teaching of the Roman pope in matters of faith or morals. Although not officially defined as a dogma until 1870, in practice it had become generally accepted in the Roman Catholic Church, though in differing degrees and not without dissent. The common statement observes that *"Whatever one may think about the appropriateness of the term 'infallible,' it points to the unavoidable issue of the faithful transmission of the gospel and its authoritative interpretation, guided by the Spirit"* (page 23, emphasis added).

The Problem of Language and Culture

Christ's command to spread the gospel into all the world and to the end of the age led to unforeseen problems. Translation into different languages is difficult because often other cultures do not have precise equivalents for biblical terms.

How could one help an Eskimo understand the significance of the phrase "Lamb of God" when he or she may have only seen pictures of lambs? (Some missionaries substituted the words "baby seal.") Was that an infallible translation? How do you convey the idea of *sin* where the nearest equivalent word is mistake?

A missionary from a South African area once said to me, "Paul, we'll never make good Lutherans out of these people, for the subtleties of sixteenth-century Germany theology are incomprehensible to their ways of thinking. But they make wonderful Christians!" This is another way of saying that the church has both the obligation and the authority to formulate its faith in such language and concepts that it can be understood and, through the working of the Holy Spirit, be appropriated by anyone in his or her own cultural thought-forms. By what authority can we translate lambs or seals?

The Process of Certification

If the answer seems self-evident, what office or procedure certifies that such reformulations retain the essence of the apostolic gospel? Lutherans have no churchwide instrument for doing this.

At the 1963 Helsinki Assembly of the Lutheran World Federation (of which not all Lutheran churches in the world are members) an attempt was made under the theme "Justification Today" to restate the sixteenth-century doctrine in twentieth-century terms. All were agreed on the doctrine as found in the historic Lutheran Confessions, but the Assembly was unable to agree upon a text which would reword it in contemporary language.

Yet, in fact, such a process is continuously going on in local parishes everywhere. A seminary president once said to me: "The simple, pious faith of my Norwegian grandmother, while adequate for her salvation, would never suffice for the spiritual and intellectual needs of my university grandson." He was not saying that his grandson would have to fashion for himself some kind of Christian faith he could accept, for in the spirit of Luther's words, conscience is bound by the Word of God and informed by the Holy Spirit. But he was saying that Word would have to be said in words of the grandson's world. How does one certify whether the word-finding is the work of the Holy Spirit? I recall an elderly synod president who decided he should stand for reelection despite the opinion of many that he should retire. "What can a child of God do when he feels God's hand on his shoulder?" he asked. I felt like telling him to check again who is on the other end of the hand! But discerning the voice of the Spirit in the clamor of competing voices isn't that simple; that's why we have hundreds of divided groups in the body of Christendom.

Vatican I—The Context

It was to a great degree this felt need for a clear-cut teaching authority which led to the 1870 announcement of papal infallibility. Why had this not happened prior to 1870 since the authority had been generally accepted in Roman Catholic circles over a considerable period prior to that time? One reason was the inroads made upon religious beliefs in general since the Renaissance and the period of Rationalism which followed. Reason and science were attacking the claims of the church and demanding a higher allegiance from "intelligent" people. A dogma was needed to buttress the teaching authority of the church. The papacy was not suddenly grasping for more power, but was anxious that the faith not be eroded by the ideas of the day. The world was becoming secular. It was beginning to put more trust in medical cures and all the other scientific discoveries. That was threatening to a church which had not been accustomed to having its teachings questioned. There were other factors, but this one is singled out because a century later the second Vatican Council was speaking to different political and intellectual circumstances.

Vatican I—The Dogma

The dogma on papal infallibility is highly conditioned. It is restricted to certain very narrowly defined teachings in which the pope is gifted with the same infallibility which Christ bestowed on his church. The Council stated that absolute infallibility is proper to God alone and that the infallibility of the pope is limited. Quoting the common statement: "The Council taught that the bishop of Rome, as successor of Peter in the primacy, is divinely protected from error when he speaks *ex cathedra,* that is, when, 'as pastor and doctor of all Christians' and by virtue of 'his supreme apostolic authority,' he 'defines a doctrine concerning faith or morals' to be held 'by the universal Church' " (page 12). Thus, papal utterances which do not meet these criteria are not infallible although in popular understanding they may be regarded as such. As stated previously, there is no official list of infallible pronouncements.

Some Clarifications

The dogma does not claim that the pope is protected from error at all times and thus is unlike other human beings. Infallibility is not a permanent property attached to him as a person. Nor is the pope given an authority independent of that of the church as though he were not a member of the church, but somehow above it. A contrary impression may be given by the statement that his *ex cathedra* definitions are "irreformable by themselves . . . and not by reason of the agreement of the church." We are told that what is intended here is that the formal approval of the bishops in a juridical way is not a condition of infallibility. On the other hand, it is asserted that the acceptance of the church as a whole will never be lacking since the same Holy Spirit which preserves the church in truth has been at work in the formulation of the papal pronouncement. (To some Protestants this might seem like going around in a circle or begging the question.)

Another important distinction has to do with the use of the term *irreformable.* This should not be so construed as to exclude further reformulation or reinterpretation. The Catholic participants refer approvingly to the assertion in the common statement that "the formulas of faith are historically conditioned and are therefore subject to revision according to circumstances of particular times and places . . . that the doctrine of infallibility itself may need to be reinterpreted and newly expressed, so that its enduringly valid theological insight may better appear" (page 43).

Infallibility as a Charism

In both Vatican councils, the term *charism,* that is, a special gift of grace, was attached to papal infallibility. In his study on this subject, Kilian McDonnell says the pope is "under the influence of the Spirit (1 Cor. 12:7), who is manifesting himself in the service of the whole church" (page 285). The gift of the Spirit is made visible when the pope ministers to the whole church in defining matters of faith and morals. Having the charism of truth (or infallibility) guarantees the assistance of the Holy Spirit, but this is not considered a type of magic.

The operations of the Holy Spirit can be obscured by human vanity, his power can be checked and hindered by apathy and pride. Nor does the infallible guidance of the Holy Spirit mean that the definition will be opportune, or be cast in the most fortunate of theological language, or be unmixed with unworthy motives. "The special charism he exercises corresponds to the special relation he has to the whole body . . . he defines infallibly in relation to the church. Apart from it he has no charism" (page 285). Even the assistance of the Holy Spirit has limitations!

Vatican II—The Dogma

While standing by the Vatican I pronouncement, Vatican II produced some important reinterpretations of it, which as stated in the *Reflections* of the Catholic participants in this dialogue, brought "new aspects to the fore." It is best to summarize in their own words:

"1. Vatican II made it clearer than had Vatican I that the infallibility of the pastors (pope and bishops) must be related to the . . . 'sense of faith' possessed by the entire people of God. The popes and bishops are infallible insofar as they are assisted in giving official expression and formulation to what is *already* the faith of the Church as a whole. This theme of Vatican II underscores what is implicit in the assertion of Vatican I that the pope has no other infallibility than that which Christ conferred upon the Church.

"2. Vatian II saw the infallibility of the pope as closely connected with that of the college of bishops. Indeed, when it described the infallibility of the Roman pontiff, it referred to him as 'head of the college of bishops,' a phrase not used in . . . Vatican I. This suggests that normally, when he defines a matter of faith and morals, the pope should be expected to consult his fellow bishops and proceed in a collegial manner. . . .

"3. Vatican II pointed out that while no antecedent or subsequent *juridical* approval by the Church is necessary for the exercise of infallibility, the assent of the Church can never be wanting to an authentic definition 'on account of the activity of that same Holy Spirit, whereby the whole flock of Christ is preserved and progresses in unity of faith.' . . . This observation, together with Vatican II's emphasis on the *sensus fidelium* (sense of faith), puts into proper context the assertion of Vatican I that papal definitions are irreformable . . . (by themselves and not because of the consent of the church).

"4. Vatican II placed the teaching of the pope in the context of a pilgrim church. His definitions of faith will reflect the situation of a church whose task is 'to show forth the mystery of the Lord in a faithful though shadowed way, until at last it will be revealed in total splendor.' . . . In other words, such definitions will inevitably suffer from a *certain obscurity.*

"5. Vatican II recognized that the Church, insofar as it is an institution on earth, is always affected by human finitude and sinfulness . . . , failings that may leave their mark even on the most solemn acts of the highest magisterium. Even while true in the *technical* sense, a dogmatic statement may be ambiguous, untimely, overbearing, offensive, or otherwise deficient.

"6. By its ecumenical orientation, Vatican II gave rise to the question: Will infallibility be able to *serve the purpose* for which it is intended without far more consultation with Christian communities not in full union with Rome?

"7. Vatican II called attention to the fact that 'in Catholic teaching there exists an order or *hierarchy* of truths, since they vary in their relationship to the foundation of the Christian faith.' . . . This important principle suggests the possibility that authentic faith in the basic Christian message may exist without explicit belief in *all* defined dogmas . . ." (pages 44 and 45, parentheses and emphases added).

The Current Intra-Catholic Debate

The Catholic participants add that "The state of the doctrine of papal infallibility at the end of Vatican II is not to be taken as the last word on the subject (page 45). This fact is well documented in two study papers: *Moderate Infallibilism* by Avery Dulles and *The Reformation and the Infallibility Debate* by George Lindbeck. Presumably most Catholic theologians accept the Vatican II stance on papal infallibility in generally traditional ways of thinking. There is a second group which advocates what is called "moderate infallibilism." It is this position which Avery Dulles explains and espouses. A third articulate, but much smaller, group believes the term *infallibility* has lost its usefulness and should be abandoned. George Lindbeck's study deals in depth with the sharp debate between the last two groups highlighted by the well-publicized dispute between two distinguished European Catholic theologians, Hans Küng and Karl Rahner over the former's book *Fallible?* in which Küng rejects the dogma. Carl Peter, in a paper which quotes extensively from the correspondence between these two men, spells out the *issue* in Küng's words (with whose analysis Rahner agrees): ". . . you [unlike Küng] presumably will not be able any more now than formerly to admit that even a solemn papal or conciliar definition could (though not necessarily 'must') in principle be not merely 'historically' restricted, limited, inadequate, dangerous, one-sided, mingled with error and therefore open to correction, but—measured by the Gospel itself—downright erroneous" (page 160, brackets added).

The two agreed to disagree. Rahner stated that his conscience forbids him to be a higher authority than the church and therefore able to reject solemn papal or conciliar definitions as mistaken. Carl Peter notes that both men would object to a unilateral attempt on the part of Roman authorities to resolve the issue, but that shortly thereafter, the Roman Congregation for the Doctrine of the Faith issued a statement (which had been confirmed by the pope) which rejected Küng's position.

Implications of This Debate

Carl Peter agrees that the last word on the subject has not been spoken. He lists three conclusions:

"1. The resolution of this theological debate among Roman Catholics about the meaning and grounds for the dogma of papal infallibility is not within sight;

"2. . . . this lack of consensus among Roman Catholics poses problems for ecumenical efforts aimed at bringing the two traditions represented in this bilateral consultation closer together;

"3. . . . the differences between Catholics remaining unresolved, progress may nevertheless be made toward greater unity if theologians in the traditions of Trent and Augsburg can arrive at something of a consensus about the degree of confidence Christians can have regarding their belief in the final and unsurpassable character of God's revelation in Jesus Christ."

Moderate Infallibilism

The analysis of moderate infallibilism given by Avery Dulles is virtually required reading for a comprehension of the intra-Catholic debate on papal infallibility. It provides a basis for sympathetic understanding of the teaching for Lutherans and others, who nevertheless will still find problems with the terminology and some ambiguities in the reasoning. It may also help Lutherans to sort out their own difficulties in formulating equivalent concepts to pursue the same essential objective.

Dulles writes: "The moderate infallibilist position includes two traits. In the first place, it affirms that the pope is infallible or at least that he has on certain occasions a charism that may not too deceptively be called infallibility. Second, the position asserts that papal infallibility, being limited, is subject to inherent conditions which provide critical principles for assessing the force and meaning of allegedly infallible statements" (pages 81–82). He adds that it might hold some interest for Christians outside the Roman Catholic tradition "who are convinced that the gospel cannot stand in the absence of all *propositional truth*" (cf. Lindbeck: page 82, emphasis added).

Infallibility as a Faith-Claim

According to Dulles, infallibility has a certain plausibility for Christians who believe that God somehow provides means for the church to remain in the truth of the gospel till the end of time. The means may not only include the canonical Scriptures, but also the pastoral office without which the Christian community would not be adequately protected against corruptions of the gospel. "The pastoral office is exercised for the universal church by the bearer of the Petrine office (which means, for Catholics, by the pope)" and "that the pope is equipped by God with a special charism (or grace of office) for correctly interpreting the gospel;" and "Authoritative pronouncements from the Petrine office that are seriously binding on all the faithful must have adequately certified truth, for there could be no obligation to believe what could probably be error" (page 83).

The Limitations and Conditions

In the light of the creaturely condition of all human teachers, Dulles believes, it would seem unreasonable to presume that the popes, or other office holders in the church, would be miraculously enabled to speak the truth on all questions, regardless of the effects of human historicity and sinfulness. Hence discernment is needed on the part of the faithful to determine whether a given statement is protected by the charism of infallibility. He lists the conditions mentioned earlier in this chapter, adding other points. A definition would be invalidated by any circumstances that would deprive the pope of his freedom and rationality—such as, a severe mental illness. George Tavard is quoted as declaring that the pope "must embody the Church's unanimity, which is not reached by obedience to one man's opinions and decisions but by free and mutual consultation and discussion in the spirit of the gospel. Papal encyclicals which do not embody this unanimity are theological documents with no claim on the allegiance of the Church's members" (page 88). Dulles adds that definitions which authentically correspond to the charism of the papal office will find an echo in the faith of the church; if not, it could mean that some of the necessary conditions for an infallible act had not been fulfilled.

Infallibility as Adequately Certified Truth

Dulles' use of the phrase "an adequately certified truth" (page 83) quoted earlier now becomes somewhat perplexing. He asserts that "adequate investigation of the sources of revelation is a true condition for an infallible teaching" (page 91). This view was proposed by a minority at Vatican I. Dulles comments that Vatican I did not rule out the view of most theologicans since the Middle Ages that it is possible for a pope to fall into heresy or schism, and that it is not easy to determine what deviations amount to heresy or schism. "Hence in some cases it could be doubtful whether the pope were validly defining . . . if grave and widespread doubts were to arise . . . the definition would have to be treated as dubious, and hence as not canonically binding. This consequence does not appear to me to be disastrous to the whole concept of infallibility" (page 92). Later on he refers to a quotation from Vatican I in a recent statement of the Sacred

Congregation for Doctrine to the effect that the hidden mysteries of God "by their nature so far transcend the human intellect that even after they are revealed to us and accepted by faith, they remain concealed by the veil of faith itself and are as it were wrapped in darkness" (page 93). Dulles adds, "Dogmas must be seen as human formulations of the word of God, formulations not undialectically identified with the revelation they transmit. Thus it is possible that one and the same faith may be expressed in formulas that stand in tension with each other—indeed, that seem contradictorily opposed. . . . The doctrine [of papal infallibility] as formulated by the Councils, is a limping human effort to articulate a mystery that defies clear expression" (page 93).

Dulles then turns to the presuppositions by which the participants of Vatican I were influenced when the dogma was formulated, and asks whether, however valid they may have seemed at that time, the church *today* does not view the issue from different premises, at least to some extent. He seems to say yes. In his opinion ". . . the vagueness of the Council gives very large scope for interpreting what is really involved when 'infallibility' is referred to. . . . It may happen that these terms will eventually be rejected as being excessively burdened with the conceptuality and polemics of a bygone era. . . . In the interests of the historical continuity and the identity of the Roman Catholic communion, I believe that the key terms of Vatican I should be salvaged if possible" (pages 96–97).

But what happens to the idea of infallibility as a charism for pronouncing "adequately certified truth"? I gather that what is meant is a special work of the Holy Spirit within the limitations of human mind and spirit which nevertheless can elicit trust, and is effective in conveying the gospel. Yet such truths are always subject to testing and further unfolding. The line between this and the Lutheran understanding of the *indefectibility* of the church gets much dimmer in this interpretation.

The Obligatory Force of the Dogma

Dulles sums up by remarking that many practicing Catholics, especially in the under-forty bracket, feel grave misgivings about the three statements from modern times that have been formally declared as divinely revealed—the Immaculate Conception, the Assumption of the Blessed Virgin, and papal infallibility itself. He lists five attitudes: (1) acceptance as unquestionably true and as obligatory upon all under pain of excommunication; (2) acceptance as true and necessary, but reinterpreted in ways that would probably have surprised those who wrote the statements; (3) acceptance as true, but without confidence that any present interpretation is the right one; (4) conviction as true in some sense, but too unclear and peripheral to affect good standing in the church, and (5) belief that the pope and the Council exceeded their rightful powers, and hence that these dogmas, even if true, have no binding force.

Dulles finds the fourth position most satisfactory. With regard to papal infallibility, he does not believe that it provides an easy and sure access to the truth in matters that are otherwise obscure. But he feels that the dogma is meaningful, focusing attention on the real importance of the papacy as a *center* of doctrinal leadership for the whole church. He is convinced that the occupants of the papal office *do* enjoy special assistance from the Holy Spirit and privileged means of access to the tradition of the whole Catholic community of churches, and that the infallibility of the universal church and of the worldwide body of pastors *comes to expression in a singular way* in the definitive teaching of the Roman pontiffs. However, he says, papal infallibility is unquestionably a problematic doctrine, even for many Catholics, and is rather remote from the core of the gospel.

Anathemas, Dulles suggests, should be reserved to those teachings which, in a given situation, destroy the *basic* stance of Christian faith.

The Significance of Moderate Infallibility

I repeat that this interpretation of the dogma is *not* that officially held by the Roman Catholic Church and probably is held currently by a relatively small (though influential) number of Catholic theologians. It is given extended attention, however, because Lindbeck and others in non-Catholic circles regard it as a potential basis for overcoming the *barrier* this dogma has become for Christian unity. Lindbeck defends moderate infallibilism as a legitimate option which perhaps alone can preserve the essential *intent* of Vatican I. Remember, the intent was to preserve the faith from the drift toward reason and secularism as the better way of life. He speaks of "the greatest crisis now confronting, not only organized

Christianity, but all the institutions in our world." He is referring to "the increasing polarization between rigid authoritarians and those who are alienated from all authority, from all stable institutionalized communities."

Authority as a Functional Necessity

Lindbeck believes that the new meaning is by no means wholly discontinuous with the old. "If one does not think so much in terms of abstract concepts but of function, it becomes evident that both traditional and moderate infallibilism have to do with maintaining the unity of the church" (page 14). He distinguishes between old style, absolutistic *authoritarianism* and a *functional* authority which is necessary to enable any institution to survive. "What is now needed is a non-authoritarian authority, an authority with which one can disagree and debate, but which nevertheless must be listened to and taken seriously. It is this requirement to listen and take seriously what a central authority says which generates a community of discourse; and discourse, when it involves genuine communication, is the fundamental unifying activity. . . . Discord cannot take the form of breaking off communication, of leaving the church. Criticism, though allowable and sometimes mandatory, must remain loyal. . . . It is this attitude of loyal opposition which moderate infallibilism authorizes" (page 115).

Does This Approach Relativize Truth?

Lindbeck's solution is based on a somewhat sophisticated understanding of language. In the introductory chapter, I pointed out a distinction between what is factual and what is held to be true. Lindbeck uses the term *intrasystemically infallible*. As I understand it, there are some core "truths" in Christianity which cannot be reversed or distorted without destroying the identity of that religious tradition historically known as *Christian*. "From the point of view of *faith*, there seems to be something objectively, propositionally and infallibly true about, for example, the affirmation that 'Jesus is Lord' (1 Corinthians 12:2) or 'God was in Christ reconciling the world unto himself' (2 Corinthians 5:19) . . . such affirmations, as well as many others, cannot be false within any recognizably Christian language system. They are intrasystemically infallible, that is, they are infallible within the circle of faith. This kind of infallibility, it should be observed, does not characterize only Christian affirmations, but is also attributable to the central assertions of non-Christian religions and of comprehensively articulated philosophical positions. Such assertions are guaranteed to be true by the whole language system or faith perspective of which they are a part. Their truth, in other words, is inescapable for those who employ the language in which a given faith is articulated'' (page 109, emphases added).

I had to read this two or three times before it made sense to me, but it does. What I believe *must* be true (or in a sense infallible) for *me,* else I could not believe it. The same is true of an entire believing community such as the Christian church. Even agnostics and atheists who scoff at faith live in or by some form of it. Existence as such makes no rational sense but is *accepted,* something *given* with all of its mysteries, conditions, and limitations. Don't all faith systems share certain broad philosophical truths, imposed on them by the language?

The Connecting Link

The implication of all this is that old-style authoritarianism threatens rather than strengthens the unity of the church, and that traditional views of infallibility render a disservice: they reinforce authoritarianism and are incredible or unintelligible. Still, authority is necessary. A Christian could not accept as true what he or she considers opposed to Jesus Christ. ''In the theological realm, therefore, acceptance of certain starting points or premises requires an assurance that, at the very least, these are not irremediably opposed to the gospel, . . . that they are in this sense infallible'' (page 117).

The Practical Possibilities of This View

Lindbeck concludes by noting that while moderate infallibilism offers considerable possibilities for convergence in Lutheran and Roman Catholic views on the subject, the remaining differences ''are not trivial.'' The moderates ''. . . retain the historic Roman conviction that only the communion united around the Petrine See is indefectibly the visible body within which the Church of Christ subsists. That Church of Christ subsists also in other communions, but not indefectibly, and their teaching offices are therefore not infallible, not exempt from ultimately serious error. Lutherans cannot accept such a view of any concretely identifiable church, including their own, without repudiating the Reformation. . . . This disagreement does not require either side to view the other as opposed to *the truth which is in Christ,* but it does mean that while Roman Catholics believe that their church will forever be preserved from such errors, the heirs of the Reformation can only hope and pray that this will be true of their own churches—and also that of Rome. These differences in degree of assurance are not trivial. . . . Yet there seems to be no reason why they should now prevent full communion. In the contemporary situation, providing other questions are resolved, Roman Catholics and Lutherans can live together in one church even though the first believe, and the second simply hope and pray, that the magisterium of the united fellowship will be preserved from irretrievable error. What the Catholics assert in this respect, the Lutherans need not deny, although they cannot themselves affirm it'' (page 118, emphasis added).

This conclusion of Lindbeck's (with which not all Lutherans would agree) deals with a question which is as he notes, ''for Roman Catholics, not for Lutherans, to answer'' (page 119).

Lutheran Headaches

Thus far we've been looking mostly at Catholic problems on *infallibility,* since Lutherans don't like to use the term. Yet Lutherans, too, reject the idea that any one can define Christian faith as he or she chooses. We've alluded to this subject when referring to the difficulty of precisely defining the term *gospel.* In the dialogue, an effort was made to identify some Lutheran equivalents of infallibility. The work was presented in the form of theses. The theses cannot be quoted in full here for lack of space, and I must say that for me the theses fall short of their objectives. The theses center upon the infallibility of God who relates himself to his creation of his Word which—according to the Scriptures—is the agency of creation, of God's self-disclosure to his creatures, of his invitation to his people, and of his work of redemption and reconciliation in their midst. Where the Word of God is proclaimed and the sacraments administered according to Christ's command, there we may be confident that God acts to invite his people. Lutherans cannot understand why one responds to, and another rejects, the grace of God, but continue to assert that God wills the salvation of all, and that his action in his Word is authoritative and efficacious. Where Christ is, in Word and Sacrament, there is also the church. The confessions stress the actual proclamation of the gospel and administration of the sacraments, and not merely an abstract correctness of doctrine. The Word is authoritative and efficacious because it is God who speaks and acts in the Word. The sacraments are efficacious because God acts in them. Neither Word nor Sacrament have inherent qualities which make them effectual. Neither church nor ministry possess inherent or independent power of survival. All depend upon the presence and action of God.

This leaves a lot up in the air. How does one tell when a teaching is authentically derived from the gospel? The Lutheran Confessions say that one must constantly test them with the gospel as found in the Scriptures; but human beings, all claiming the guidance of the Holy Spirit, disagree on many points of doctrine. We're in exactly the same bind as Roman Catholics. The paradox is that faith leads us to be certain about Christ and the gospel, but not about *everything* the church says in its attempts to make theological affirmations about them.

A Personal Aside

As mentioned earlier, majority vote is not a guarantee of truth. Thus I am skeptical of any *ultimate* doctrinal authority of church conventions. A few years ago, a Lutheran church body adopted a doctrinal statement which was made binding upon all pastors and teachers in that body (although the vote was far from unanimous). Is there much to choose between? The choice is between positions voted in by theologically untrained laity and some partially informed pastors or the pronouncements of Roman pontiffs who collected the painstaking studies of theologians over years of time. For example, the dogma on the Immaculate Conception followed six years of intense worldwide discussion in the Roman Catholic Church. Of course, the view that majority votes do not always necessarily reflect the mind of the Holy Spirit presumably applies also to ecumenical councils as well as Vatican councils. Yet a lack of faith in the guidance of the Holy Spirit leaves the church without any credibility at all. Some kind of teaching authority is essential. So I am left with the same kind of attitude toward the status of convention or council decisions that George Lindbeck attributes to Roman Catholic moderate infallibilists in their evaluation of papal pronouncements.

Parallel Problems

Lutherans have their counterpart to Catholic tensions in the current standoff between those who ascribe to the Scriptures as inerrant, and those who ascribe to the gospel as witnessed by Scripture. The latter hold that the gospel establishes its own authority, namely, "its truth becomes known and its authority acknowledged only upon being heard through the Word, received in the Sacraments, and believed through the power of the Spirit. Neither scriptural inerrancy nor, even less, the infallibility of the church's teachers, teaching offices, and doctrines are the basis of the Christian's confidence. All these may err, but not the Gospel of God's unconditional mercy in Jesus Christ to which the biblical writings are the primary witness." This divergence of viewpoints is a major cause for the fact that world Lutheranism numbers over one hundred churches.

How Do We Come Out?

Although full agreement was not reached, the progress made was impressive. In their *Reflections* the Catholic participants express their sadness over their inability to announce full agreement, but are encouraged by the large measure of agreement that does exist. In fact, they find it difficult to specify the exact point at which, in fidelity to the respective traditions, disagreement is necessary. They remark that some Lutherans, while denying what they recognize as infallibility, come close to affirming what some Catholics teach by that term.

One Key Issue

The Catholic participants have come to express papal infallibility in terms of *promise, trust,* and *hope*. This is a far cry from an authoritarianistic or juridical approach. They are bewildered why Lutherans do not seem to have enough trust in the power of the grace of God to guide the Roman pontiff in fulfilling the Petrine function. Lutherans respond that their lack of trust is not in the power of God's grace, but in the absence of any scriptural or historical grounds for the claim that it centers on any one person or office rather than on the universal church. But the important point is that the two groups did not regard this difference as central to the gospel or necessarily divisive.

Practical Implications

Can anything be done pending full agreement on the subject, which probably is many years off? This dialogue group believes so. Among suggestions on the Catholic side are the possibilities of reviewing, rescinding, or "committing to oblivion" past condemnations of Luther and Lutheran teachings on this subject; taking a new look at the Lutheran Confessions—especially, *The Augsburg Confession*—with a view to reinterpreting them in a new context. This context would highlight their catholic dimension and perhaps recognize them as valid expressions of the church's teaching; the Lutheran Confessions could then become an instance of *magisterial mutuality* (consultation in teaching). It is asked whether some form of institutional relationship might be discovered to express magisterial mutuality and would correspond to the converging state of the two traditions. Since some sacramental sharing with the Orthodox who do not accept papal infallibility is authorized by Rome, might some similar arrangement be made between Roman Catholics and Lutherans?

On their side, Lutherans ask (1) whether their churches should not admit that the polemical language used traditionally to describe the papal office (such as Antichrist) is inappropriate and offensive today; (2) whether Lutherans should not, participating in a movement toward a common witness in our day, be willing to consult with Roman Catholics in framing doctrinal and social-ethical statements; and (3) whether Lutherans should move to develop closer institutional relationships with the Roman Catholic Church in respect to teaching authority which would be expressive of the converging state of their respective traditions.

Caution and Admonition

The group concludes by pointing out that all grounds for continuing division have not yet been removed; more work is to be done; reactions to their findings must be considered; and that agreement among theologians does not imply consensus of the churches they represent. Yet they insist that the common ground that was discovered points the way *forward* to significant changes in the lived relationships between Lutherans and Roman Catholics. Past oppositions can be overcome, they assert, only as the churches become more engaged at all levels "through theological reflection, study of the scriptures, worship, mission, and pastoral care, in a search for convergence along the lines developed in the work of this dialogue." Amen!

By now you may have your fill of the word *authority*. For several chapters, the discussions have kept circling back to the word and all its problems. That is natural, however, because that was the chief problem of the dialogue—how to establish which teachings are right when teachings differ. If we could establish a common authority, then all disagreements could be appealed to the authority.

As the discussion now stands, the Lutherans appeal to the gospel message in the Scriptures as their authority, but interpret that message with a certain assumed authority. The Catholics see a process starting in the Scriptures with the apostles. They ascribe their authority to that process and see it continuing down to today.

Dilemmas

1. Which is more true—an individual's beliefs or the church's teachings?
2. Which is more fallible—the individual's beliefs or the church's teachings?
3. Is the gospel infallible?
4. Can an infallible gospel come through a fallible church to a fallible individual?

DISCUSSION

Suggestions for a Discussion on Teaching Authority

- The group could discuss the following case study:

  A debate was arranged between two groups in a religion class. One side represented the idea that the church had to determine what is a Christian belief and what is not. The other side said that the individual must decide, that is, that the person's beliefs could not be declared anathema by the church.
  As participants, which side of the debate would you prefer to be on? Is there a middle ground? Is there a way in which the work of the Holy Spirit through the church's teachings must be one pole of authority, while the work of the Holy Spirit in the lives of individuals is another pole and the two are in healthy tension?

- The group could discuss how the church could be sure its teachings were consistent with the gospel and how the individual could come to have more confidence in the church's teachings than in his or her own ideas.

- If there are differences of belief in the group, pick one of the differences and discuss how the holders of the differing opinions could find out which was right. That is, what is the ultimate authority?

- Have the group choose a belief they all agree to, and then have each person tell why she or he believes it is right and true. List the reasons on the chalkboard. For example, one may say it just makes sense to me (this authority is reason). Another may say the Scriptures teach it; another, the Holy Spirit through the reading or the interpretation of the Scriptures; another, the church; and another, I feel it to be true (which might be emotions or instinct). After the reasons have been written on the chalkboard, have the group check how many similarities there are in the authorities they list.
- The group could complete the study by planning a time when they could worship at both churches involved and meet afterward for brunch and discussion.